Praise for *Re*FOCUS

Have you ever wondered if there was hope for the American church? Read this book and rejoice! Focus on the Family's Jim Daly and this book are God's gracious gifts to a hungry church. Daly "gets it," and in this important book he reminds us in clear, winsome language what it *really* means to be a Christian. Please read this book and be a part of what God is doing in our generation.

ERIC METAXAS, *New York Times* bestselling author
of *Bonhoeffer* and *Amazing Grace: William Wilberforce
and the Heroic Campaign to End Slavery*

Everyone needs to read *ReFocus*. It's a bold call with a humble approach to cultural transformation. Jim Daly refocuses our attention from the success of winning cultural battles to the significance of serving the wounded on the battlefields of life. This book is long overdue. And I'm so glad Jim Daly had the courage to write it. What a refreshing and desperately needed message! Don't miss it.

LES PARROTT, PHD, www.LesandLeslie.com,
author of *You're Stronger Than You Think*

Jim Daly has written an indispensable handbook for Christians called to defend the truth in the public square. He raises the questions we need to ask ourselves if we are to represent Christ in a worthy manner.

TOM A. COBURN, MD, United States senator from Oklahoma

In his life and in his ministry, Jim Daly embodies three extraordinary qualities: an unassailable Christian faith; a spirit of hope and joy that flows from it; and a willingness to engage anyone, anywhere, in honest dialogue about the central issues of life. His book reflects the man. This is a wonderful, engaging testimony that transcends the differences that divide Christians and speaks to the task we all share in common — witnessing Jesus Christ to a world that never needed him more than it does now.

CHARLES J. CHAPUT, O.F.M. CAP., Archbishop
of Philadelphia

The tension of being "in the world but not of the world" has always been an issue in the church. Our relationship to those who are sick has been a source of tension from Matthew and his friends till now. Jim Daly gives no slick answers from church canon law — it's not that easy. He does give perspective. *ReFocus* is a read that provokes contemplation.

TOM NELSON, pastor, Denton Bible Church, Denton, Texas

With compassion and conviction, *ReFocus* will challenge the priorities of your faith. What I appreciate most about this book is that I know Jim Daly strives each day to live the message. As a husband, father, and leader, he reflects God's heart.

TED CUNNINGHAM, pastor of Woodland Hills Family
Church, Branson, Missouri, and author of *Young and in Love*

*Re*FOCUS

Living *a* Life *that* Reflects God's Heart

JIM DALY WITH PAUL BATURA

ZONDERVAN
BOOKS

ZONDERVAN BOOKS

ReFocus
Copyright © 2012 by James Daly

Requests for information should be addressed to:
Zondervan, 3900 *Sparks Dr. SE, Grand Rapids, Michigan* 49546

Zondervan titles may be purchased in bulk for educational, business, fundraising, or sales promotional use. For information, please email SpecialMarkets@Zondervan.com.

ISBN 978-0-310-36893-9 (softcover)
ISBN 978-0-310-33178-0 (audio)
ISBN 978-0-310-33177-3 (ebook)

Library of Congress Cataloging-in-Publication Data

Daly, Jim, 1961–
    ReFocus : living a life that reflects God's heart / Jim Daly with Paul Batura.
        p. cm.
    ISBN 978-0-310-33176-6 (hardcover, jacketed)
    1. Christian life. I. Batura, Paul J. II. Title.
BV4501.3.D353   2012
248.4–dc23   2012025408

All Scripture quotations, unless otherwise indicated, are taken from The Holy Bible, New International Version®, NIV®. Copyright © 1973, 1978, 1984, 2011 by Biblica, Inc.® Used by permission of Zondervan. All rights reserved worldwide. www.Zondervan.com. The "NIV" and "New International Version" are trademarks registered in the United States Patent and Trademark Office by Biblica, Inc.®

Scripture quotations marked NIV, 1984 edition, are taken from The Holy Bible, New International Version®, NIV®. Copyright © 1973, 1978, 1984 by Biblica, Inc.® Used by permission of Zondervan. All rights reserved worldwide. www.Zondervan.com. The "NIV" and "New International Version" are trademarks registered in the United States Patent and Trademark Office by Biblica, Inc.®

Scripture quotations marked MSG are taken from *THE MESSAGE*. Copyright © 1993, 2002, 2018 by Eugene H. Peterson. Used by permission of NavPress. All rights reserved. Represented by Tyndale House Publishers, Inc.

Scripture quotations marked NLT are taken from the Holy Bible, New Living Translation. © 1996, 2004, 2015 by Tyndale House Foundation. Used by permission of Tyndale House Publishers, Inc., Carol Stream, Illinois 60188. All rights reserved.

Scripture quotations marked ESV are taken from the ESV® Bible (The Holy Bible, English Standard Version®). Copyright © 2001 by Crossway, a publishing ministry of Good News Publishers. Used by permission. All rights reserved.

Any internet addresses (websites, blogs, etc.) and telephone numbers in this book are offered as a resource. They are not intended in any way to be or imply an endorsement by Zondervan, nor does Zondervan vouch for the content of these sites and numbers for the life of this book.

Published in association with Ambassador Literary Agency, Nashville, TN.

Cover design: Extra Credit Projects
Cover image: Getty Images
Interior design: Beth Shagene

*To all past, present, and future heroes of the faith,
who sacrifice in order to ensure
that their hearts beat in sync
with the heart of the One
who came to show us the way—
our Lord and Savior, Jesus Christ.*

Remind the people to be subject to rulers and authorities, to be obedient, to be ready to do whatever is good, to slander no one, to be peaceable and considerate, and always to be gentle toward everyone.

At one time we too were foolish, disobedient, deceived and enslaved by all kinds of passions and pleasures. We lived in malice and envy, being hated and hating one another. But when the kindness and love of God our Savior appeared, he saved us, not because of righteous things we had done, but because of his mercy. He saved us through the washing of rebirth and renewal by the Holy Spirit, whom he poured out on us generously through Jesus Christ our Savior, so that, having been justified by his grace, we might become heirs having the hope of eternal life.

THE APOSTLE PAUL,
TITUS 3:1–7

The fall of the human race starts not with an action but with an attitude. Not with an act but with a sneer.

DR. TIMOTHY J. KELLER, "THE GOSPEL
ACCORDING TO GOD" (SERMON SERIES)

Christianity says that the trouble with men and women is in their heart, in their ultimate power of vision and understanding. It is not that they are partially wrong, they are all wrong; they are looking in the wrong direction, they are blinded at the most vital point. The organ that keeps them going is itself in trouble—the heart. So our Lord puts this great emphasis upon "first," and "heart," and "eye" and this is just a pictorial way of saying that what the human race needs is not just to be improved a little bit here and there ... they need to be radically changed.

D. MARTYN LLOYD-JONES,
THE KINGDOM OF GOD

So let the reader who expects this book to be a political exposé slam its covers shut right now. If only it were all so simple! If only there were evil people somewhere insidiously committing evil deeds, and it were necessary only to separate them from the rest of us and destroy them. But the line dividing good and evil cuts through the heart of every human being.

ALEKSANDR SOLZHENITSYN,
THE GULAG ARCHIPELAGO

Contents

Contents

1

Time *for a Change*

Since this new way gives us such confidence,
we can be very bold ...
   Therefore, since God in his mercy has given
us this new way, we never give up. We reject all
shameful deeds and underhanded methods.
We don't try to trick anyone or distort the word
of God. We tell the truth before God, and all
who are honest know this.

2 CORINTHIANS 3:12; 4:1–2 NLT

MY EYES WERE FIXED ON THE FACES OF MY TWO SONS, THEIR eyes huge with wonder. Trent and Troy were getting their first look at the magnificent Mount Rushmore. I drank in this perfect scene — my boys, ages nine and eleven, struck speechless by the immense white sculpted mountains honoring four of our nation's great presidents. I had been anticipating this moment mile after mile, and now my heart swelled with gratitude — gratitude for these two young men God had entrusted to Jean and me, gratitude for this great country, and gratitude to the God who had given me this moment.

My wife, Jean, and I had spent months planning this vacation and had driven our fifth wheel from Colorado Springs to the famed but desolate outpost in the scenic Black Hills of South Dakota. Even though I absolutely love my role at Focus, it was great after a particularly tough spring to finally get away from the rigorous office routine and reconnect with the boys at the start of their summer vacation. I had my smartphone in my pocket; I had made a conscious decision to stay away from work and had asked my assistant to refrain from calling me except for dire emergencies.

I moved from studying the faces of my sons to studying the faces of Washington, Jefferson, Roosevelt, and Lincoln, contrasted against the crystal-clear blue sky that called my eyes heavenward.

And then my phone rang.

I looked down and recognized the number. It was the office calling, but given the remoteness of our location, the signal was weak. I attempted to answer it, only to quickly lose the call. After repeated attempts at reconnecting, I found a tiny spot where the phone held a signal. I had to almost stand on one leg and lean to one side in order to hear the caller. The news was disheartening.

Several months earlier, our Focus on the Family team had planned an event with TOMS. This corporation was founded on a novel concept: for every pair of TOMS shoes purchased, the company donates a pair to a needy child. When I first heard about what they were doing, I was intrigued. "The goal isn't how much money you make but how much you help people," founder and CEO Blake Mycoskie told the *New York Times* in 2009. *Impressive*, I thought. *I'd love to learn more.*

Blake's concept sparked an idea at Focus. We arranged to host a special event to bring attention to the work that Blake and his colleagues were doing. I believed that his story would inspire other Christians to act on their faith and help others in need. We wanted to highlight the great work of TOMS and tell our friends how they could join the mission of putting shoes on the feet of impoverished kids. We envisioned the possibility of giving away as many as a half million shoes through the program.

The night finally arrived, and I interviewed Blake in front of an audience of more than fifteen hundred guests on a summer evening in Southern California. As we left California, we were humbled by the success of the event and excited to see the response to the broadcast, which had yet to air across our radio network.

But now, standing in South Dakota, I was told that TOMS was no longer comfortable with their association with Focus. Blake had just posted a blog about Focus on the Family, and his words, read to me by our vice president of communications, Gary Schneeberger, saddened me. Earlier in the week, Blake and his company had been chastised and petitioned by homosexual advocates, demanding that he apologize for speaking at our event.

What did Blake say in his blog that incited such a strong reaction one week after the interview? He suggested that if he had known what we stood for as a ministry, he wouldn't have agreed to speak at our event. The topic was grist for the blogosphere, especially at sites promoting homosexual rights. I was most saddened by the level of vitriol heaped not only on Focus on the Family but also on Blake and his colleagues at TOMS by those with whom we have ideological disagreements.

A few days later, Blake and I talked on the phone. I greatly respect and appreciate him and understand the pressure exerted by people in his own organization to distance himself and TOMS from Focus. I tried my best to listen more than talk and didn't try to strong-arm him. Because we had already taped the program and had it in our possession, we had the ability to ignore Blake's wishes and air the program. In fact, given the brewing controversy, it would have generated significant publicity and ratings for Focus. But after talking with Blake, I agreed not to air the radio program. It grieved me to think of the great opportunity we had to help kids — but because of the criticism of a vocal minority, we wouldn't be able to do so. I'd hoped that our partnership with TOMS would be a positive experience of working with those in the business sector, yet our past efforts to be a voice of truth within our culture had alienated so many people that this opportunity to put shoes on the feet of children was squelched.

What happened?

How did we arrive at such a point that an organization like Focus on the Family is deemed unfit by some in our culture to help children in need simply because we hold to what we believe are biblical mandates about marriage and family?

Something is wrong.

But we already knew that.

We're living in tough and confusing times. We see the brokenness of the world, the inevitability of disappointment, the relentless cycles of heartache.

We see the ugliness inside our culture — the absurdity of seemingly really smart people doing really unwise things — and we find it to be distasteful and downright destructive. We see conflict and controversy growing on a daily basis, pride and power plays, and the sad realization that money, sex, prestige, and power seem to drive the passions of people on all sides of the issues.

If you are like me, you want to do something about it — but what?

There must be a better way.

There *has* to be a better way.

Perhaps you, like many followers of Christ, have been pouring your heart and soul into the task of helping others, either individually or collectively. Maybe you've also been doing your best to help solve the problems of this world, whether social, political, economic, or environmental.

But there's a problem.

In the process of jumping in, rolling up your sleeves, and getting busy working toward solutions, you've discovered that the great divisions in our culture are creating boundaries that we cannot seem to cross. The clash of values has enraged so many, has so alienated citizen from citizen and believer from believer, that even in our efforts to alleviate suffering and help those in need, we are viewed with suspicion or even contempt.

You've also realized that *you* don't always act like a Christian — and that all too often your heart bends more to the world's ways than to the ways of Jesus.

Do you see what that means?

You're actually part and parcel to the problems of the world.

So am I.

And that's the problem beneath the problem.

The Right Attitude

As Christians, we're irritated when we see other Christians behaving badly. We grow frustrated when we see people inside the church treating others unkindly. Whether it's the infighting of partisan politics or disputes over how to strategically engage with the culture, or even theological arguments of various stripes, we don't always get along with each other in the Christian subculture. We also don't seem to have much patience for candid and respectful discussions when disagreements spring up. In fact, we're quick to jump to conclusions and even quicker to criticize our own people when they define the problems, or the solutions, differently than we do.

Let me give you an example.

During a recent interview with Marvin Olasky of *World* magazine, I was asked about the same-sex marriage debate within today's culture. The discussion took place in front of students from King's College inside New York City's Empire State Building. I simply acknowledged what the facts support. I shared with Mr. Olasky that among younger Americans, same-sex marriage is gaining acceptance and that we're rowing against the tide. I affirmed that we have God's design on our side, as well as social science research that affirms the wisdom of traditional one-man/one-woman marriage. Yet given the obvious paradigm shift among the younger generation, I noted that we're fighting an uphill battle of demographics. Given the facts, how should the church respond to this growing divide? Are we ready for the day when a majority of people disagree with the multimillennium-old definition of marriage? If not, shouldn't we be ready for it?

Once the excerpted interview was published, several of my Christian associates were upset with me for making such an observation. In response to my attempt to bring perspective and share what the Lord had laid on my heart, some people ridiculed me — yes, these were my fellow Christians! Some perceived my comments as weak, akin to waving a white flag of surrender. Some even accused me of caving in to supporters of same-sex marriage. One supporter even went so far as to write in a private e-mail, "Never have I been so embarrassed to be affiliated with Focus on the Family!"

To be clear, I was not suggesting that Christians throw up their hands and accept the reality of same-sex marriage. I was simply trying to express what so many are struggling with: How do we navigate the coming age and culture in the manner and methods commanded by Jesus? How do we disagree with certain principles within culture without being hostile in our attitude? If our current methods are failing to stem the tide of public acceptance, shouldn't we consider the possibility that the Lord is calling us to engage in a different way?

Since assuming my role as president of Focus on the Family, an international ministry dedicated to helping families thrive, I've had many chats with the Lord about what He is calling me to communicate on His behalf. These haven't been audible conversations, of course, but I have clearly felt His leading and direction during my prayer times these last seven years. Here is the essence of what He's been telling me — and what has motivated me to sit down and write this book.

I believe the Lord wants us to get our hearts ready for spiritual battle. Yes, He's concerned about the practical problems of the world because behind every problem there are people. Real people. People He created. People He loves. People with whom He desires to be in relationship with on a daily, 24/7 basis. So it's critically important to engage the world and do what we can to alleviate suffering, bring comfort, and allow the Lord to use us to accomplish these things on His behalf.

But He is especially concerned about the condition of our hearts. He's concerned about what motivates you and me. He's concerned about what gets you out of bed in the morning. He's just as much, if not more, concerned about *why* you care about something as He is with *what* you care about.

When I examine my life, I'm often struck by the fact that I'm all too often more in love with the heartbeat of the culture than I am with the heart of God Himself. If this weren't true, I wouldn't get upset when I receive a stinging e-mail criticizing me for something I believe the Lord wanted me to say — the comment at King's College, for example. If I truly cared more about God's ways than the world's ways, I wouldn't grow anxious or despondent when my candidate of choice doesn't win an election or when someone or something infringes on my religious liberties. Of course setbacks of this nature disappoint us, but they shouldn't paralyze us.

Let me ask you what I asked the students of King's College: *Are you ready?*

Are you ready to engage the culture with winsomeness and with great patience and confidence? Are you ready to endure the slings and arrows of both friend and foe, knowing that you stand solidly on principles that are forever, on words that are rooted in Jesus Christ? Are you ready to play — even if you're quite sure you're not going to "win" — at least not win according to the world's standards?

And here is an especially hard question: Are you ready to play Jesus' way — to see those living outside God's will not as opponents to conquer but as people loved by God — people who need to experience His love, possibly even through you?

If you're anxious and worried about the culture, do you doubt that the Lord has His hand firmly on the wheel?

Are you ready to examine what only you and the Lord can see?

Are you ready to "do business" with the state of your own heart, mind, and soul?

At the very outset, you should know that this isn't a book about what's going badly in the culture, but rather one about how Christians should respond to it. Are we doing the right things for the right reasons? Are we more concerned with shaping the debate than we are with shaping and refining our own attitudes toward the world? I'm reminded of the old song "Let There Be Peace on Earth." Do you remember it? "Let there be peace on earth," the song begins, "and let it begin with me." Or perhaps we should consider the words of a song more familiar to today's culture: "I'm looking at the man in the mirror. I'm asking him to change his ways."[1]

Let's be honest with ourselves. Sometimes we're more concerned about God making right the wrongs of the world than we are with cooperating with Him to help us first right the wrongs of our own hearts.

If we're going to help win people to the heart of Jesus, it's critical that our own hearts are wedded to His.

Change begins inside our hearts. This is the message Jesus pounded into the heads of the religious leaders of his day.

Physician, Heal Thyself!

When we read through the Gospels, we quickly discover that Jesus is repeatedly dealing with the religious people and forcing them to confront the shape of their hearts toward the sinful world. Consider the bold charge in Luke:

21

"But to you who are listening I say: Love your enemies, do good to those who hate you, bless those who curse you, pray for those who mistreat you. If someone slaps you on one cheek, turn to them the other also. If someone takes your coat, do not withhold your shirt from them. Give to everyone who asks you, and if anyone takes what belongs to you, do not demand it back. Do to others as you would have them do to you.

"If you love those who love you, what credit is that to you? Even sinners love those who love them. And if you do good to those who are good to you, what credit is that to you? Even sinners do that. And if you lend to those from whom you expect repayment, what credit is that to you? Even sinners lend to sinners, expecting to be repaid in full. But love your enemies, do good to them, and lend to them without expecting to get anything back. Then your reward will be great, and you will be children of the Most High, because he is kind to the ungrateful and wicked. Be merciful, just as your Father is merciful."

LUKE 6:27–36

To be candid, I struggle with these instructions. This behavior doesn't come naturally to me. And from what I've seen in the way people treat those with whom they disagree, I think all of us struggle with these instructions. These are God-focused and supernatural teachings, and the flesh, even subtly, considers this guidance beyond reach. Of course, on our own, it is — but not if we allow God to grab hold of our hearts. Not if we allow Him to mold and shape us in a way that compels us to live lives that reflect His heart, not ours. The New Testament urges us to live quiet lives so we can live in peace. It also reminds us to pray for those in authority over us, including those in government. You'll note that within the Scriptures we see no distinction of person or ideology. "Give back to Caesar what is Caesar's and to God what is God's" is how the gospel writer Mark (12:17) recorded Jesus' instruction. As Christians, we have an obligation to live under secular authority, as long as in doing so, it doesn't compromise or violate God's law.

Do you get what this means? To live in this fashion requires us to lay down our own egos, put away our prideful self-interests, and set aside our own expectations. It also means that if we truly embrace this perspective, then we're likely to run into difficulty and encounter awkwardness and conflict.

So when we encounter this conflict, what are we to do?

Here is the great challenge: we are always called to express our concerns and opinions in a respectful and thoughtful manner. I don't see any teaching in the New Testament that allows us to cast aside our godly character to gain some victory, regardless of how grand the prize. In other words, the ends do not justify the means. If we Christians attempt to fight a battle with only the goal to win in mind, then we have sold out and do not have the character of Christ. We all want to teach our kids about character. We repeatedly tell them it isn't about winning or losing but how you played the game. But when it comes to this arena for adults, whether it is in the church or the political theater, do we apply this same principle? What is in our hearts toward the opposition?

I try to remember that the world is constantly watching Christians, wondering whether we truly believe what we preach and profess to be true. In fact, there are some non-Christians who will form an opinion of Christ Himself through an interaction with a person who claims divine allegiance. I have deliberately tried to apply this truth to every aspect of my life.

I am grateful beyond words that Jesus came to eradicate the distance between me and God that was caused by my sin and to invite me into a relationship with God. In the Bible, He instructs me on how to interact with those around me — the believer, the nonbeliever, the godly, the ungodly, those in authority, the religious rulers, and others. I am seeking to reconnect with the heart of God and refocus my efforts to reach a world that does not know His heart.

And may I be candid, especially since we're going to spend some time together over the course of these next pages?

When I look at the culture and the needs of this world, my heart is breaking. I look out, and I am moved toward those who fight Him, reject Him, or, even worse, ignore Him. This is why I am compelled to share this message with you. May the Lord bless and guide your thoughts as we confront one of the greatest tests of our time — the challenge of refocusing our efforts on living in such a way as to invite others to experience the love of Jesus and come to know Him as their personal Savior.

2

The Clash *of Two Worlds*

Submit yourselves for the Lord's sake to every human authority: whether to the emperor, as the supreme authority, or to governors, who are sent by him to punish those who do wrong and to commend those who do right.

1 PETER 2:13–14

Peter and the other apostles replied: "We must obey God rather than human beings!"

ACTS 5:29

THE SMALL SLIP OF PAPER HAD BEEN SITTING NEXT TO MY telephone for months. It contained the name and phone number of a well-known homosexual activist, someone I had wanted to talk with for several months. Life had gotten very busy, and I had delayed calling him, convincing myself that I would do so as soon as life quieted down.

Each time I saw the piece of paper, I felt the Lord encouraging me to call soon, that the "right moment" would never come, that I was probably just procrastinating and feeling a bit uneasy to reach out to a person who believed very differently from the way I believed.

I finally got up the nerve and made the call. We set up a time to have coffee near my office. The meeting was warm and cordial, and although we found that our views were different on several vital issues, I felt that the Lord was right in the middle of our conversation. I could feel His presence at the table. We didn't shy away from our differences but talked openly and honestly about how differently we saw God's design of human sexuality. But for the majority of our time together, we talked like any two people would in the middle of a busy week, two weary travelers on life's long highway taking a moment to step back from the responsibilities and pressures of the day. As our initial conversation drew to a close, I felt the Holy Spirit prompting me to share a thought with my new friend. "You know" — I addressed him by name — "God loves you just as much as He loves me. Do you know that?"

There was silence across the table as this man dropped his head and looked off to the side. He wasn't able to say a word in response. But he didn't have to say anything. I saw tears in his eyes. It was a poignant moment for both of us. Stereotypes had been shattered. Neither of us had changed the other's mind, but that wasn't what this meeting was all about. The reminder of God's love for him had overwhelmed him. It surely wasn't my style or the choice of my words that connected with him and moved him to tears. It was the influence of God.

Try as we may to run away from God and even deny His existence, He'll never stop pursuing us. He is infinitely patient. He'll never give up on us.

As I walked across the parking lot to make my way back to the office, I gazed at the front range of the Rocky Mountains. The sun was setting and the sky was ablaze in orange and blue. I had just experienced a holy moment. In fact, in all my years at Focus, I don't think I had ever experienced an exchange as powerful — or as simple — as the one inside that coffee shop.

Within minutes of arriving back at the office someone asked me about the visit. The person was suspicious of my overture to this homosexual activist and feared that by meeting together, I was in jeopardy of compromising my principles. Furthermore, he was afraid that I might wind up embarrassing the ministry if word got out that the president of Focus on the Family was drinking coffee with this man. I was taken aback. I told him I was surprised that a fellow believer would think that showing Jesus' love to someone would somehow compromise or thwart God's ultimate plan. In retrospect, the exchange was especially painful because of the sheer magnitude and poignancy of the experience. Here I had just come from one of the most beautiful moments in my twenty-plus years of ministry, and this person, who knew me well, was suspicious of the exchange. I listened to the objections. Then I said, "You know, I understand where you're coming from, but I don't think we have the authority to choose with whom we share the gospel." I was specifically thinking about Jesus' words in Luke's gospel: "If you love those who love you, what credit is that to you? Even sinners love those who love them" (6:32).

This encounter also made me think about the lesson Jesus taught Simon the Pharisee about sin. In the middle of a dinner at Simon's house to which Jesus had been invited, a woman with a "bad reputation" began anointing Jesus' feet with expensive perfume.

Then he turned toward the woman and said to Simon, "Do you see this woman? I came into your house. You did not give me any water for my feet, but she wet my feet with her tears and wiped them with her hair. You did not give me a kiss, but this woman, from the time I entered, has not stopped kissing my feet. You did not put oil on my head, but she has poured perfume on my feet. Therefore,

I tell you, her many sins have been forgiven — as her great love has shown. But whoever has been forgiven little loves little."

LUKE 7:44 – 47

Looking back on my experience, I am struck by this irony: when I had left earlier in the afternoon to meet this person for coffee, I had braced myself for the inevitable cultural clash that awaited me. After all, theologically and socially speaking, we were coming from two very different worlds. The meeting confirmed the differences we had, to be sure, but at the end of the day, I experienced more of a clash with my Christian brother than I did with the homosexual activist! The exchange highlighted the fact that when you're trying to live as Jesus lived, you will inevitably encounter resistance along the way — both inside and outside the church walls.

Historical Perspective

There is a tendency to believe that today's challenges are more difficult than yesterday's. This "cultural clash" seems to some to be a modern-day development, which is clearly not the case. In fact, many people are quick to point to the 1960s as the beginning of the cultural slide. While there is a tinge of truth to the cultural revolution of that era, to blame that decade for all of the modern-day ills is shortsighted. Cultural clashes have posed an ongoing challenge for Christians from long ago and especially in the early church.

As the fourth century turned toward the fifth, the decline of the Roman Empire was accelerating. Although the empire wouldn't officially fall until AD 476, the handwriting was on the wall. From political corruption to economic tensions to rabid immorality, the deterioration was incremental but also cumulative. Aurelius Augustinus (more commonly, Saint Augustine of Hippo, or simply Augustine), the bishop of Hippo Regius (modern-day Algeria), saw what was ahead. He was concerned that the imminent collapse of the ruling establishment would be blamed on Christians. Although he knew that no political force could bring about the demise of the one true faith, Augustine was, at heart, a pragmatist. If persecution could be avoided, he was committed to doing what he could do to prevent it.

To be fair, Christianity was, in fact, contributing to the empire's increasing instability and irrelevance. For the commoner, life under Roman rule was hard, harrowing, and hopeless. Early death was not unusual, if you even made it out of childhood. But the introduction of Christian theology following the death of Jesus in AD 33 — the teaching that life and all of its accompanying pain is but temporary and eventually redeemable — was like balm on a burn. Early in the fourth century, Rome's emperor, Constantine the Great, had converted to Christianity. As a result of this conversion, regarded by most historians as the turning point of the early church, citizens now felt free to openly practice their faith. The change was dramatic. It would be impossible to overestimate the influence and impact of a Christian heading up the Roman Empire. With Constantine's issue of the Edict of Milan in AD 313, a new era of religious tolerance was ushered in, a change that loosened the chains for many faith expressions but especially for the fledgling Christian movement.[1]

As the empire's influence waned toward the latter part of

the fourth century, government leaders were pressing church officials to take a more active role in the empire's politics, hoping their sheer numbers and influence might save the sinking ship. Church officials, including Augustine, refused to cooperate in any significant manner. The bishop and his brethren were committed to drawing a clear distinction between the role of the church and the responsibility of the state. Fearing that the empire's demise would be blamed on people of faith for not fully cooperating, the bishop put to paper his perspective on the need for maintaining separate and distinct roles. Hoping that a convincing justification would stave off the inevitable persecution that would result in continuing political instability, he wrote these words:

> Accordingly, two cities have been formed by two loves: the earthly by the love of self, even to the contempt of God; the heavenly by the love of God, even to the contempt of self ... In the one, the princes and the nations it subdues are ruled by the love of ruling; in the other, the princes and the subjects serve one another in love, the latter obeying, while the former take thought for all.[2]

Reflecting on the benefits of reforming and melding the theological with the philosophical, Augustine stated that "the princes and the subjects serve one another in love, the latter obeying, while the former take thought for all."

By the time Augustine arrived on the scene and was appointed bishop in 395, the notion that governmental support of Christianity was good for Christianity had been fully ingrained in Christ's early followers. Many of these same people also believed that this cozy relationship should be nurtured, expanded, and — most definitely and especially — defended, regardless of the pain or the price.

What struck many as strange about Augustine was his departure from this conventional wisdom. Indeed, Augustine saw things very differently. Although he was not openly antagonistic in spirit, he believed it was beneficial to maintain autonomy between church (City of God) and state (City of Man) interaction. In fact, he believed it was possible for church and state to be too close for comfort, and he concluded that distance or at least distinctions were healthy and appropriate.

Consumed by this passion to articulate the distinctions between church and state, Augustine continually impressed on his fellow believers a timeless point, the essence of which remains practical for Christians today: even if the earthly city fades and falters, the heavenly city will not. Christianity's message and purpose are spiritual and do not provide the material for political talking points. The sustainability and essence of its message is not tied to either government endorsement or persecution. Ideally, faith complements and informs our politics and policies. In contrast, our policies and politics should be reflective of our faith. It is to be a symbiotic, though autonomous, relationship — not antagonistic or wholly separate. This was Augustine's perspective, and he expended great energy into trying to explain this to the powers of the day.

The Two Kingdoms

The doctrine of the two kingdoms was introduced into my thinking as a teenager. My mother died when I was just nine;

my father, who had abandoned our family years earlier, died when I was twelve. But prior to my mother's death, I watched her put in long hours as a waitress. Come what may, she was providing for our family. As I grew up and assumed responsibilities, I learned from her that it was up to me to do my duty in the earthly kingdom. In high school, it was my football coach and other godly men from whom I learned the characteristics of a godly man and essentially began to understand my role in the second kingdom — the arena of my faith and my commitments as a Christian.

By the time I graduated from college and met my wife, Jean, this idea had been firmly ingrained. It was clear and straightforward for me, even simple. I was a resident of two places, earth and heaven. While on earth, I was to be a good citizen, and in whatever I did, I was to do it joyfully and bring glory to God in the process. I understood I was supposed to be working for God, and I saw work as vocational and that which we are created to do. I have always enjoyed my various jobs and have tried to excel at each position. But I've also wanted to do my work with purpose, mission, and joy. Vocation as joy is the heart of it, and I relish this as an idea given by Christ Himself.

Sadly, in my lifetime, I've witnessed a growing separatist strain in the American Christian church, one that I believe is misapplied and regrettable. Some people conclude that any reference by Christians to anything even remotely "political" is out of bounds. In recent years, many of my fellow Christians and I have engaged in debating critical areas of social policy, including hot-button topics such as marriage, abortion, adoption, and foster care. Ardent supporters of strict separation — a minority, to be sure — interpret our involvement at best to be foolish and at worst to be unbiblical.

To my friends who hold to this point of view, I respectfully but strongly disagree. For example, any discussion on the definition of marriage incites strong emotional reactions these days. And those of us in the orthodox Christian community understand that many in contemporary culture see this issue very differently and hold to deeply passionate views on the subject. We understand that on this matter in some circles it is unlikely we will have a meeting of the minds. Nevertheless, this difference of opinion does not deny us the privilege of championing a principle we hold dear, especially since it is our Christian faith that motivates us to support what we believe to be God's blueprint for human relationships. In the last half century, progressives have exercised their own rights of cultural engagement, aggressively championing sweeping changes on numerous levels. As I shared with the homosexual man over coffee, although I may disagree with the same-sex agenda, I certainly don't begrudge homosexuals the right to engage the process.

What would you do?

I believe government is God given, and that the aim of government is to restrain evil. It may also be true that this point of view is conservative by nature and seemingly out of step with modern trends and mores. Nevertheless, I believe that prudence dictates this approach: this side of the divide is Caesar's, and that side of the divide is God's. Perhaps this is why I have always loved Thomas More's statement, "I die the king's good servant, and God's first."[3]

The Blurring of the Lines

At the time Dr. Billy Graham and Ronald Reagan first met in 1953, both men were rising stars, one in the pulpit and the other in a pseudo-political role. Mr. Reagan was on the verge of signing a lucrative deal as a corporate spokesman for General Electric, a move that would not only earn him a good living but also put him in everyone's living room for the next eight years. Still, Dr. Graham's future appeared even brighter. The great Los Angeles crusade in the fall of 1949, held inside a hot Ringling Brothers circus tent, made Billy Graham a household name all across the nation. By the hundreds of thousands people were flocking to stadiums and arenas to hear his lilting Carolina drawl. With enthusiastic and robust evangelical fervor, the tall and lanky Graham was sparking spiritual revival all throughout post–World War II America.

That first meeting between Graham and Reagan was memorable for another reason. They had gathered in Dallas to help raise funds for a retired film actor's home. On the dais with the two men was Dr. W. A. Criswell, the senior pastor of Dallas's First Baptist Church, one of the country's largest and most influential Protestant congregations. The forty-four-year-old Criswell was known for strong opinions, both in and out of the pulpit. With Graham looking on, the Southern Baptist clergyman was true to form. Movies were of the devil, he told Reagan. Graham was incredulous. All the while, Mr. Reagan listened politely. He then proceeded to share with Criswell his perspective on the positive aspects of the movie industry and the number of good, wholesome films that were being made in Hollywood. To his credit, the fiery pastor absorbed the winsome retort. When Reagan concluded, Criswell spoke. "I'm going to start going to some movies," he replied, "and I'll tell my congregation that it's not a sin to see certain types of movies."[4]

The incident greatly impressed Dr. Graham, who marveled at his new friend's keen ability to navigate cantankerous criticism. "Ron had not only changed a man's mind," Graham wrote, "but he had done it with charm, conviction, and humor —traits I would see repeatedly as I got to know him."[5]

These same traits and shared interests kept Reagan and Graham close through the years. The close ties also put the evangelist in a tough spot when Mr. Reagan was running for president in 1980. Just prior to the Republican Convention, Dr. Graham crossed paths with Reagan during a trip through Indiana. The polls were tightening, and Mr. Reagan said he especially needed help in North Carolina — Billy's home state. Would Graham be willing to say a kind word about him? It was the first time he had ever asked for political help, and he only now did so because it could well make the difference in the race.

"Ron, I can't do that," Graham told him. "You and I have been friends for a long time, and I have great confidence in you. I believe you're going to win the nomination and be elected President. But I think it would hurt us both, and certainly hurt my ministry, if I publicly endorsed any candidate."[6]

Mr. Reagan told Graham that he understood, though his aides appeared frustrated. Still, just like that, the tension between the two quickly faded.

This wasn't the first time Dr. Graham had been forced to navigate the confluence of politics and religion. Over the years it had become a predictable and in many ways unavoidable source of tension for the evangelist, and how could it not have been?

In the summer of 1952, Dwight Eisenhower, then a candidate for president, had asked Graham if he would be willing to add a spiritual tone to Eisenhower's campaign speeches. Now a friend and admirer of Eisenhower, who had been the commander at the Supreme Headquarters of the Allied Powers in Europe, Dr. Graham agreed but shared with him that his political preferences must remain private. Throughout the summer, the future president confided in Dr. Graham that he had "gotten a long way" from the devoutness of his youth.[7] When pressed, he shared with his friend that he had become disillusioned with faith years earlier and that their developing friendship had sparked a renewed spirit.

When asked what had taken him away from the church, Eisenhower surprised Graham. He told him he'd been bothered to see many preachers spending little time teaching God's Word and instead focusing on social or secular matters.

For Dr. Graham, the church's business wasn't just the exposition of the gospel and the defense of orthodox doctrine and evangelism. It surely wasn't less than that — but it was far more too. Christians, he believed, were called to be active in every area of life and culture. Years later, Dr. Timothy Keller, senior pastor of New York City's Redeemer Presbyterian Church, summed up the challenge to find this delicate balance:

> What does this [striving for balance] mean? It means that any simplistic Christian response to politics — the claim that we shouldn't be involved in politics, or that we should

"take back our country for Jesus" — is inadequate. In each society, time, and place, the form of political involvement has to be worked out differently, with the utmost faithfulness to the Scripture, but also the greatest sensitivity to culture, time, and place.[8]

What Graham, and later Keller, had come to see as a natural way of life, theologians struggled for centuries to understand, manage, and even define. Saint Augustine called it the "two kingdoms."[9] Martin Luther identified it as the "two spheres."[10]

Balancing the Two Worlds

The Bible is full of examples of religious men who attempted to influence a secular culture. Joseph became prime minister of Egypt and was greatly used by God. Daniel held a high position in Nebuchadnezzar's government in Babylon, and yet he remained faithful to God. The apostle Paul, in his letter to the Philippians, references believers "who belong to Caesar's household" (4:22), indicating that they were working at the highest levels of earthly power.

As something of an aside, and to be fair, the fusion of the two kingdoms in Old Testament times didn't always go smoothly. We read that when Abraham and Lot arrived in the area around Sodom, Abraham, concerned about becoming too closely associated with the city, chose to live outside its walls. Lot wasn't concerned and "pitched his tents near Sodom" (Genesis 13:12). As we know, he survived, but his wife and some other family members did not. As it is with all of life, finding the balance is the key — and the challenge.

A Two-Track Solution

Thus far, I have focused on the political side of the conflict of the "two kingdoms," but the world of politics is just one element of the "other" earthly kingdom. There are plenty more. In some ways, we've become so obsessed with the "political" angle concerning the balance of engaging the "two spheres" that we've forgotten that human nature regularly corrupts many other good things of this earthly kingdom — things like love, sex, money, and possessions.

In fact, far more men and women are lost to these vices than to the abuse of politics. As such, many Christians, especially orthodox ones, struggle with practicing what they preach, even to the point of leading double lives.

Theoretically speaking, we understand that in order to lead meaningful and robust Christian lives, we must sometimes get "dirty" or encounter perspectives that are contrary to the teachings of Jesus. This makes good sense to us — until we encounter a real-life opportunity for direct engagement with some person or some group holding an alternative viewpoint.

I was posed with just this challenge regarding personal engagement last year. As many of you know, Focus on the Family has been engaged in a thirty-six-year battle to overturn *Roe v. Wade*, the Supreme Court decision that legalized abortion in all fifty states. The campaign hasn't been easy. It's had its share of ups and downs. I take my hat off to all who have labored with dedication and sacrifice to advance the pro-life cause over these last four decades. Over the years, those of us within the pro-life movement have done great things to incrementally improve a very evil reality. Babies have been saved. Hearts have been changed. But because it doesn't appear we're going to reach our ultimate goal of eliminating abortion any time soon, I asked our friends and supporters a practical and realistic question: *How do we save more children right now who would otherwise be aborted?*

At the time, I revealed that I felt compelled to meet with abortion providers and express a challenge. For years, they've told us they want to make abortion "safe, legal, and rare." We will never agree that it's safe or that it should be legal. But I proposed meeting with them to say, in essence, "You want to make abortion rare? Tell us how."

I was suggesting a two-track approach in the battle to protect life. Our desire is to see the day when every life is seen as sacred. In the meantime, I cannot stop thinking about the children we're losing right now. We will not compromise our convictions. But how do we save more children who would otherwise be aborted?

The vast majority of those within the pro-life community understood and even appreciated my modest proposal. One writer, Jim, was representative of the hundreds of letters I received in response.

Dear Jim,

The challenge you have laid out is the very thing that those who advocate and support abortion fear the most, yet it is something we must pursue. By doing so, we will be able to share our message with love and conviction. We will be able to communicate the need to take ownership and responsibility for the choices and positions we take. We will be able to emphasize that we are all accountable for the

value of and protection of all human life. This will make
those who sit across the table from us uneasy, to be sure,
but it will allow us to lay the seeds for transformation to
take place one heart at a time. As hearts begin to change,
it stands to reason that attitudes and behaviors toward
abortion will begin to change as well.

Thank you for steadfastness and faithfulness on such
a defining issue.[11]

Yet I received criticism from others for making such a proposal. The objections in the form of e-mails, letters, phone calls, and face-to-face conversations came mostly from friends who, like me, are opposed to abortion. I took their criticism seriously. Some of them called me naive, soft, an appeaser. And they were not shy about explaining why they had come to this conclusion. Why, they charged, would I waste my time with the other side? Why would I be willing to flirt with evil and legitimize abortion groups like Planned Parenthood and NARAL with a meeting? But the most thoughtful and challenging response came from Ryan.

Dear Jim,

While I appreciate considering different approaches,
I can't help but feel that the presupposition is so tragically
flawed. Where is the evidence that abortion apologists want
abortion to be "rare"?

This approach (offered numerous times over the past
several years) also diminishes what pro-lifers claim is the
inherent nature of abortion: evil. Where else do we try to
merely diminish evil and pat ourselves on the back because
we've attempted to find common ground? While we engage

*in one-sided acquiescence, pro-abortion politicians and the
abortion industry pour hundreds of millions into assuring
that abortion on demand becomes codified on state and
federal levels.*

*I can't help but think the church will decades from
now have to issue inexplicable apologies, just as numerous
denominations did for slavery, for not doing enough to
counter this present evil, for not having loved people enough,
for not being the salt and light that was so desperately
needed while millions perished.*

*Abolitionists didn't settle for slavery reduction; many
risked their reputations and their very lives to call for the
end of a system of human degradation, not its continuation
through appeasement and mutual understanding.*[12]

I appreciate the sincerity with which Ryan offered his perspective. While some abortion rights activists truly are uncon-
cerned about the senseless deaths of pre-born children, my
research and conversations with individuals from these opposition camps suggest many *are* deeply troubled and riddled
with guilt. I have personally met with people inside the abortion industry, and some of them are distressed about the con-
sequences of legalized abortion. Although they do not agree
entirely with me, they do believe fewer abortions would be a
good goal.

As for Ryan's assessment regarding the purity of the abolitionist's motives and strategy, there is evidence to suggest otherwise. The abolition of slavery was never a zero-sum game. In
Great Britain, William Wilberforce led a fifty-year campaign
punctuated by a series of incremental legislative actions that

reduced slavery in various forms, year by year. In the United States, prior to the passage of the Thirteenth Amendment in 1865, slavery was also abolished over several years, according to territorial and politically negotiated terms.

I've always maintained there is wisdom in taking a two-track approach: (1) continuing the campaign to overturn *Roe v. Wade* and lobbying for the passage of pro-life legislation, such as laws that require parental notification and ultrasound screenings, and (2) sitting down with representatives from groups such as Planned Parenthood to talk about promoting adoption and lobbying for the inclusion of ultrasound machines — exploring practical ways of trying to save the lives of pre-born children.

The Apostle Paul Deftly Navigated the Two Worlds

The road map for our way forward is found in the Bible. Widely considered to be the architect of the early Christian church, the apostle Paul, a man on a mission to spread the good news of Jesus Christ, regularly engaged in debates with political authorities. How did he do it? Did he stubbornly refuse conversation and turn his back in apathy and indifference? Hardly! In fact, Paul was often forced to endure the unfairness of false charges brought by a conspiracy of anti-Christian Jews.

Paul's discussions with Felix, Festus, and King Agrippa give us model portraits of a Christian facing opposition and responding with respect, dignity, and humility. When Paul was brought before the Roman governor Felix to defend himself against charges, Paul began by saying, "I count myself fortunate to be defending myself before you, Governor, knowing how fair-minded you've been in judging us all these years" (Acts 24:10 MSG). He then proceeded to refute the false evidence presented against him and asked Felix to check the facts for himself.

Felix kept Paul imprisoned but refused to have him condemned or punished further. In fact, we're told in Acts 24 that the Roman governor frequently called Paul out of his cell to discuss the gospel message with Felix and his wife, Drusilla. A couple of years later, Paul remained behind bars while Felix was replaced by Festus, who inherited Paul's case. When brought before the new governor, Paul stood his ground and firmly maintained his innocence. Festus, in a politically correct attempt to appeal to his Jewish constituents, tells Paul that perhaps they should move the trial to Jerusalem (where, if Paul lived long enough to be brought to trial, enough "witnesses" could be bribed to testify against him).

In response, Paul demanded that they try him right there, accompanied by evidence against him, or else let him go. And he concluded his lawyerly speech by appealing to Caesar! This provided the too-slick Festus with his loophole, and he decides to send Paul to the emperor. Before this can happen, however, King Agrippa and his queen came for a visit to welcome and congratulate Festus on his new job. After explaining Paul's case, Festus shoved it off to Agrippa, who agreed to hear Paul in a public court. Now keep in mind that King Agrippa is the grandson of King Herod, the one who tried to kill Jesus as a baby!

Once again, Paul displayed a calm, courteous demeanor to his captor: "I can't think of anyone, King Agrippa, before whom I'd rather be answering all these Jewish accusations than you, knowing how well you are acquainted with Jewish ways and all our family quarrels" (Acts 26:2 – 3 MSG). Paul went on to recount his conversion on the road to Damascus, including his sordid past as a ruthless persecutor of Christ's followers.

Continuing to explain how he came to be there, Paul then shared about Jesus' death on the cross and resurrection. At this point, Festus interrupted Paul and called him crazy for spreading such a preposterous story. The model prisoner then called on King Agrippa's knowledge of the prophets and their foretelling of the Messiah as evidence that supported his story. Agrippa responded, "Keep this up much longer and you'll make a Christian out of me!" (Acts 26:28 MSG).

There is no doubt that Paul's testimony was firm. But does his gentle approach, as well as King Agrippa's response, stand out to you? Paul was always holding out a hand of grace to all. In this ongoing clash of the two worlds, this is our way forward. We need to acknowledge that there are issues on which we must take a stand. We must be willing to defend our faith, the sanctity of human life, and the religious freedoms that are foundational to our country's greatness. But in doing so, we must strive to imitate Paul's example of grace and deference, remembering that, first and foremost, we are citizens of a kingdom that is not of this world. We are sons and daughters of the King of all kings. It's always time to humble ourselves and love those around us, even those who oppose us.

3

Don't *Panic*

So we say with confidence,

"The Lord is my helper; I will not be afraid.
What can mere mortals do to me?"

HEBREWS 13:6

THE NIGHT BEFORE I WAS INSTALLED AS PRESIDENT OF FOCUS on the Family, I found myself unable to sleep. It's quite unusual for me to be jittery about coming events, but this particular step in my career had left me perplexed and even a bit uneasy. Of all the people on the planet, why would the Lord pick *me* to lead this worldwide ministry? By my own assessment, I was an unlikely choice.

From the perspective of family background, I was the antithesis to the organization's founder, Dr. James Dobson, who came from a stable, traditional Christian home. His father was a pastor; his mother was fully devoted to her small family. When I think of the Dobsons, I think of a Hallmark Hall of Fame television presentation. In contrast, my parents divorced when I was five. My mother died when I was nine, and my father succumbed to exposure when I was twelve. Between these losses, my stepfather was harsh and combative and ultimately abandoned the kids on the afternoon of my mother's funeral. I spent a year bouncing in the foster care system in Southern California, and the foster father I'd been living with even accused me of trying to kill him. It was a lie, of course. The man was not well. Suffice it to say, I grew up amidst chaos, strife, and dysfunction.

So, staring at the ceiling the night before the investiture into the presidency, I was struck by my own sense of inadequacy and my fear that I wasn't up to the job. I wondered whether the organization needed to be led by an individual with a storybook background. But in the darkness and quiet of the overnight hours, the Holy Spirit spoke to me. As I prayed and pondered, the words of the apostle Paul repeatedly washed over me.

To keep me from becoming conceited because of these surpassingly great revelations, there was given me a thorn in my flesh, a messenger of Satan, to torment me. Three times I pleaded with the Lord to take it away from me. But he said to me, "My grace is sufficient for you, for my power is made perfect in weakness." Therefore I will boast all the more gladly about my weaknesses, so that Christ's power may rest on me. That is why, for Christ's sake, I delight in weaknesses, in insults, in hardships, in persecutions, in difficulties. For when I am weak, then I am strong.

2 CORINTHIANS 12:7–10 NIV (1984 EDITION)

Indeed, I felt weak and ill-prepared, but God reminded me that in the history of the world He has repeatedly used simple people to carry His message. For it was in that same letter to the church at Corinth that Paul reminds us that God's glory is like "treasure in jars of clay to show that this all-surpassing power is from God and not from us" (2 Corinthians 4:7).

It became crystal clear. It's not about me. It's not about you. It's about allowing ourselves to be used — warts and all — by the Creator of the universe. By shifting our perspective, by realizing that the Lord doesn't call the equipped but instead equips the called, our anxiety and worry can fade and eventually wash away. I know what you're thinking. We all worry — and at times, it seems inescapable. But worry is a passive form of arrogance. Here's why. It's believing that you know how things are supposed to turn out. It's taking God's seat for yourself.

We don't worry because we fear God's will won't be done; we worry because we're afraid that things won't go our way.

So if you take nothing else away from this chapter, I hope you'll leave with this: As you assess the chaotic cultural scene, as you find your way forward and cultivate your faith in Jesus Christ, as you discern God's will for your life and those entrusted to your care, you must stop worrying about the outcome. We are not called to be successful; we are called to be faithful. As a famous poet once aptly put it, "Do thy duty, that is best; leave unto thy Lord the rest!"[1]

A Childlike Faith

Nearly forty years before that restless night prior to my promotion, I found myself in a much smaller bed but feeling equally alone. This time I was lying all alone in the dark and scared out of my wits. I was five years old. My father was drunk, and he was sitting in a brown corduroy chair in our darkened living room. He had a bottle of booze in one hand and a ball-peen hammer in the other, which he continued to thump on the ground in rhythmic fashion. He had already smashed a hole in the drywall and was waiting for my mom to come home from work. He announced that he intended to kill her, and by the degree of his rage, I had no reason to doubt that he meant it.

Fortunately, my oldest brother, Mike (fifteen at the time), had told me to go to my room, assuming it was the safest place for an innocent child. My other brother, Dave, had slipped out another bedroom window to get Mom from her waitressing job at the bowling alley. The two of them eventually returned with two police cars, and the ordeal was peacefully resolved. They did arrest my dad, but many of the details of that night are fuzzy. I do remember a policeman slipping into my room at one point and coming alongside my bed. "Son, are you OK?" he asked. I nodded. "Sure." I could tell he wasn't buying the bravado and looked closer at me. "OK," I admitted, "maybe I'm a little scared."

A warm, knowing smile eased across his face. "Trust me," he said. "Everything will be just fine."

Today's Culture

I think from time to time about that incident, and as I do, I recognize that there is redemption within the trauma. That scary moment has been a metaphor for my view of God and the way He involves himself with the details of our lives, both individually and collectively. It is easy to panic when troubles come. It is easy to allow the danger and evil of the world to consume us and to begin thinking that today's culture is hell on earth. It's not. It's not all sunsets and roses, obviously, but as Mark Twain once said of the music of Richard Wagner, "It's not nearly as bad as it sounds." Through every twist and turn and bad news bulletin, I continue to hear the whisper of God, who, much like that nameless policeman, tells me to trust Him. Don't panic. Everything is going to be OK.

Do you regularly hear that same voice?

Admittedly, our culture continues to announce its volatility. But if you think times have never been worse, you're simply unfamiliar with history. For example, in ancient Greece and Rome, infanticide was widespread. Babies were considered chattel — personal property on the same level as animals. Female infants were particularly vulnerable and frequently killed by being exposed to the cold and other harsh elements of the climate. Consider this horrifying letter from a husband to his wife, which was recently recovered from ancient Egypt:

> *Know that I am still in Alexandria ... I ask and beg you to take good care of our baby son, and as soon as I received payment I shall send it up to you. If you are delivered (before I come home), if it is a boy keep it, if a girl, discard it.*[2]

The spread of Christianity began to revolutionize and redeem the coarseness of ancient culture. By definition, a Christian life was countercultural. Infanticide was prohibited within Christian circles, as evidenced by some of the earliest known documents of the era, including the *Didache*, a manual for converts, which plainly states, "You will not kill [him or her] having been born."[3]

Among other reforms, Christianity helped to end the routine, evil practice of killing children; what's more, it helped change the philosophy that led to people thinking it was acceptable in the first place. Christianity affirmed the sacredness and uniqueness of every human life, a value that was foreign to many people of the day.

We seem a long way from those barbaric days, but are we? Abortion is legal in all fifty states, and nearly one million children are legally killed in the United States each year. Nearly 90 percent of pre-born children with Down syndrome are aborted each year, and more girls are killed than boys. Even more to the point, why doesn't the scourge of abortion shock more Christians? It could be that time has dulled our senses. Thirty-nine years is a long time. Has the shock of it all faded the evil of it all? Perhaps for some. But frankly, I believe one of the main reasons many people don't consider the dignity of life as a top-tier issue is this: It's different when the numbers don't have names and photographs attached to them. Instead of hearing names and seeing faces, we read and see the astronomical numbers related to abortion, which startles but doesn't shock.

Every number lost to abortion is a name known to God. If people saw the faces, as God does, if people saw snapshots of the lives that were to be, I think more would see that every child deserves a chance and has a right to life.

Other cultural norms seem to be shifting, and dramatically so. Essentially, the norms no longer apply. A child in some states can't assume that if a friend's mom is married, she is married to a man. How should we as Christians regard the kind of cataclysmic shift that we're feeling beneath our feet? Is it just one bad news bulletin after another? Should we accept it as the inevitability of cultural decline? Should we be somewhat cavalier and chalk it up as nothing new under the sun? Should we rant and rave and ridicule its author? My fear is that most of us respond to this shift with either indifference or enmity. Neither response is adequate — because to ignore the problem is akin to turning our back on the people who need help, and to respond angrily is to poorly represent the love and grace of God.

Understandably, many Christian people have been disappointed, hurt, and frustrated by the cultural dysfunction over the past five decades. It's easy to see why we panic. The majority of people know something is wrong, but not everyone agrees on what to do about it. Within the church we see three main camps these days. Can you find yourself somewhere in these descriptions?

Some want to ignore the problem and maintain the business of church as usual. This group isn't surprised at the weight of moral depravity, political corruption, and social promiscuity that permeates our culture; they expect no less from a country that has lost touch with its Judeo-Christian roots. These folks are not alarmed by losing some people along the way; after all, every battle has casualties. In this segment of believers, any talk of a "culture war" is met with either fatigue or outright disinterest. After all, didn't Jesus Himself talk about those people whose faith roots did not go deep enough to survive the storms of life?

Then we have the more traditional camp of long historic standing in which believers are quite comfortable and eager to engage the culture. Christians in this group are happy to hand out voter guides, host candidate forums, and openly confront modern-day evils — whether manifested in the form of abortion clinics or pornography stores. They enthusiastically collect signatures for ballot initiatives, such as a marriage amendment or an anti-gambling law. Many evangelical Christians are typically associated with this group. They've been called everything from "the Religious Right" to, more recently, "values voters."

And finally, we see countless Christians who aren't sure what to make of the cultural shifts in nearly every area of life. They agree that things are troubling and very much want to see traditional moral values like marriage and the sanctity of life upheld. Many of them are uncomfortable with the idea of voter guides being handed out on church property, even though they've been just as disappointed or hurt as anyone else in this clash of culture. Yet they can't pretend that nothing has changed and that things can continue in the same way.

I find myself somewhere between the second and third groups. I take literally Jesus' words in John's gospel: "My kingdom is not of this world. If it were, my servants would fight ..." (18:36). I believe we're called to engage with but not *fight* against the world with the world's tactics. And I engage, not in the hope of bringing God's kingdom to this world, but in the hope of introducing the people of this world to eternal life and God's kingdom to come.

I believe the time has come to forge a new way. For the believer, business and behavior as usual are over. For Christians, another model of engagement is emerging that is influential, creative, imaginative, and principled; it will eventually take root — first in culture, then in government and law. But in the midst of this paradigm shift, we are not to repudiate the "old ways" or carelessly discard those who have brought us to this point. Instead, the time has come to apply a fresh devotion to tradition. The time has come to adjust, draw in the new culture, and, in Ezra Pound's great words, "Make it new."[4]

Nearly everyone is in agreement that simply building bigger churches, drawing in larger numbers of people, and emulating cultural norms with coffee shops and rock-performance-caliber worship bands will not be enough to turn the tide. And time has shown that when we ask the question, "What would Jesus do?" the answer we receive will be largely dependent on who we ask.

Turning Point

In evaluating the best way forward, I find it helpful to study history. Mark Noll is considered by many scholars to be today's premier historian of religion in America. In his landmark book *America's God*, Noll makes a startling observation. According to his analysis, during the 1830s and 1840s our nation was the closest it has ever been to truly being converted. In other words, never before (or since) has there been a time of such shared Christian consensus. It was a time, Noll argues, when the society trusted the church, embracing its vision and values with little opposition or angst. Acceptance of evangelical Christianity was sweeping the country "because they [Christians] could demonstrate how their form of faith could vivify, ennoble, and lend transcendent value to the most influential ideological engines of the nation: republican political assumptions themselves, democratic convictions about social organization, scientific reasoning pitched to common sense, and belief in the unique, providential destiny of the United States."[5]

However, just as the nation was tipping toward near-complete conversion, the slavery debate began to rage red-hot. Noll suggests that our nation's leaders waited expectantly for

the Christian church to "solve" the great dilemma. Years passed
without resolution. Indeed, not only did America's Christian
leaders not solve the great slavery debate; they likely exacerbated it as both sides found theological evidence to support
their regionally based belief. In the South, Christians maintained that the Bible never condemns slavery and in fact con-
dones it in several passages. In the North, Christian leaders
defended emancipation as compatible with the spirit of the
gospel and that of a redemptive Jesus Christ. The talking and
debating continued for decades — until war came, men died by
the hundreds of thousands, and a nation was practically torn
in two. It was at that time, Noll suggests, that American Christianity changed — and hasn't been the same since.

Mark Noll makes a thought-provoking argument, but I
believe we have come to yet another critical point in American
Christendom. Will the church lead or defer to forces inside and
outside its walls? Will we Christians stand for biblical truth,
regardless of how unpopular it may be? Are we ready to endure
ridicule and persecution with grace and love? The foundations
are shaking, and although the faith will never fall, I sense that
if we are to live a life that reflects God's heart, we are going
to have to check and recheck our attitudes. As believers, are
we lurching toward selfishness, arrogance, or pride? Or are we
becoming more selfless, humble, and authentic? Are we too
quick to panic when things are not going our way?

I become frustrated when I read about individuals threat-
ening to leave America in protest. They're panicking. They see
the America they love slipping away and feel a natural urge to
re-create it somewhere else, even if it's just in their own little
world. But I don't think that's a Christian response. It reminds

me of the kid on the playground who brought the ball and threatens to bolt if the other children refuse to follow his rules. A Christian is best prepared for tough times because of the calm sense of confidence that comes with knowing the Lord is in complete control of all time and space (Matthew 6:34; Romans 8:28).

4

Fan *or Follower?*

Everyone who loves has been born of God and
knows God. Whoever does not love does not know
God, because God is love ... We love because he
first loved us.

1 JOHN 4:7 – 8, 19

My freshman year at Cal State San Bernardino got off to a rough start. On my first day of class, I encountered a professor who was enamored with the Greek philosophers Aristotle, Plato, and Socrates. He was articulate, even eloquent in his presentation. But in a moment of poor judgment on my part, although not intending to be controversial, I decided to challenge him on what I considered to be a key omission.

"What about the words of Jesus?" I asked.

In an instant his face turned red, and he unraveled right before my eyes. "There's no evidence that Jesus ever lived," he responded gruffly. "Most intelligent people know the Bible is nothing more than a myth, a compilation of stories that human beings want us to believe about a perfect man to make themselves feel better."

The exchange came as a blow not only to my ego but also to the strength of my faith and the confidence I thought I possessed to defend it. I realized just how unprepared I was to articulate what I believed in my heart about the authenticity and truth of Christianity. Though difficult, the incident caused me to dig in and study the Bible more deeply. That semester I began to read it for hours at a time, and in the process I developed a deeper relationship with God.

In short, prior to that incident with my college philosophy professor, I had been a fan of Christianity. I "got it" from an intellectual standpoint and didn't doubt all the essentials of the faith. In fact, I could have easily recited with conviction the Apostles' Creed. But I had not internalized and made the faith my own. Now, studying and reading God's Word, for the first time in my young Christian walk I began to feel my heart moving closer to Him. I was becoming a follower of Jesus — not just a fan from afar.

Not a Fan?

Kyle Idleman is the teaching pastor at Southeast Christian Church in Louisville, Kentucky, and the author of *Not a Fan: Becoming a Completely Committed Follower of Jesus*. His words strike right at the heart of this issue. "We have all kinds of funny ways to measure our relationship with God and have things that we point to as evidence," he writes, "like the fact that there is a fish on our bumper or people will talk about the fact that their grandparents went to church or that they have four Bibles in their house … Jesus doesn't want fans; he wants completely committed followers."[1]

I strongly resonate with Pastor Idleman's perspective. He is addressing the very thing I was confronted with in college. How authentic was my faith? When I was twenty-two, just prior to graduation, I decided to spend a year studying abroad at Waseda University in Japan. It was another eye-opener for me, especially related to my growing love for Jesus, as I learned about some of Japan's main religions — Shintoism, Buddhism, and Hinduism. For example, Shintoism teaches that you have to pay money for a good name so that when you die, you get closer to the Creator. It saddened me that poor people pooled their money to buy a name for their deceased loved ones. And it struck me as suspicious that you actually had to pay the priest to get the name. Again, the exposure to these religions caused me to dig deeper into Christianity. For me, the contrast between the faiths was startling and instructive.

It can be valuable to have a person or culture challenge core beliefs. The interaction with my professor forced me to dig deeper and read my Bible from cover to cover to make sure I really did believe what I claimed to believe. My time in Japan gave me an entirely new perspective on the doctrine of grace. It helped me better understand how deep God's love is for us and caused me to rejoice that unlike other major religions of the world, we don't have to pay any institution in order to draw closer to Him. Both of these instances helped me continue my transformation from mere fan of the faith to follower of Jesus.

Yet another incident overseas further solidified my personal commitment to the Christian faith. It forced me to examine my attitude and come to terms with just how authentic my personal expression of belief was.

Prior to assuming my current role with Focus on the Family, I served as vice president of its international division. At the time of my appointment in 1992, my friend and colleague Peb Jackson, along with Dr. Dobson, thought my time abroad in Japan during college was good preparation for the assignment. I was humbled by the appointment and the confidence they showed in me. I've always appreciated the way Dr. Dobson approached our international outreach. At the time we launched the division, he was concerned about falling into the trap of being the ugly American in our work outside the United States. As we began the outreach, though, our strategy was simple and highly deferential, going only where we were invited. In those first few years I traveled to China, Malaysia, South Korea, Japan, England, France, Germany, New Zealand, Australia, and South Africa, to name just a few countries. Each of those trips was eye-opening on various levels, but one stands out above the rest.

Landing on a hot afternoon in Jakarta, Indonesia, I was exhausted. I had been away from home for nearly three weeks and was eager to see Jean. My host had sent a car to the airport to pick me up — a comfortable Mercedes. Still, the luxurious transportation did little for my attitude. I slumped into the backseat and thought of my colleagues in Colorado Springs, together with their families and enjoying all the conveniences and comforts of home.

The driver slowly wound his way out of the airport and through the noisy and congested streets of the city. The smog in Jakarta is legendary. The rickshaws dart between cars with plumes of smoke billowing out. The smog was so thick that day I could taste it in my mouth. Amid the slow-moving traffic, I began to feel sorry for myself. After an hour of travel, and still only halfway to the hotel, the car came to a sudden stop. I looked to my left. Playing in a puddle of dirty black water, not twenty feet from the car, were five little boys who couldn't have been older than ten years of age. The few clothes on their backs were in tatters, and they had no shoes on their feet. Looking around the neighborhood, I wondered if they were homeless street kids, maybe orphans. And yet, despite their dire circumstances, they were dancing and singing in the mud puddle and having a grand time. Imagine — they were making boats out of Coke cans and floating them in the puddles! They looked over and smiled big, toothy grins, waving a hearty hello. My heart swelled with compassion, and I no longer slouched in the backseat of the car but leaned forward, heartily and happily waving back at them. One boy approached the window to say hello. And then the car moved forward, and they disappeared from sight. The key to this story is what the Lord was speaking to my heart. After waving good-bye, I turned my gaze back to the road, and I felt the Lord saying this to me: *They have joy with so little. Where is yours with so much?*

That serendipitous encounter took place nearly twenty years ago, but the image of those boys is forever etched in my mind. I have thought about those little boys ever since and wondered what happened to them. I've regretted not being able to help them, but the memory of their smiles has helped me. Here I was grumbling and grouchy, sitting in the back of a luxurious car taking me to my hotel. By contrast, these little homeless boys were ecstatic and on fire for life. They had nothing, at least as far as I could tell, and yet they were happy and seemingly content with their lot in life. Ever since, whenever I'm tempted to think of what I don't have but want, I think of what these needy boys received — namely, a spirit of contentment.

Although I grew up with very little and learned to get by with meager resources by doing such things as putting Kool-Aid on my cereal because we had no milk, that brief encounter on the streets of Jakarta helped cure me of the devious idols of envy and discontent. Every day the world is screaming to me that happiness can be purchased when, in fact, the best things in life are those things that money can't buy.

Telemachus: A Profile in Christian Courage

There is a danger in comparing ourselves to ancient characters, especially when it comes to matters of Christian courage. After all, when contrasted with the challenges faced by early martyrs of the faith, our challenges pale in significance, and our deeds, well, let's face it, seem dreadfully puny. But it is good to remember the giants who have preceded us because their stories can inspire and force us to reach well beyond our grasp. The story of Telemachus is chilling and offers a valuable moment from history as we evaluate whether or not we are completely sold out for Jesus and the essentials of the faith. I love this story because it reminds me that although I may be only one person — and a very inadequate one, at that — a single individual can accomplish miraculous things if God is with them. While I do not want to compare myself to Telemachus, I do want to be more like him. Let me tell you the story.

On January 1, AD 404, thousands of spectators crowded into the Roman Coliseum itching to see a good fight — a fight to the death, that is. As the bloodthirsty fans took their seats in the coliseum, dozens of gladiators steeled themselves for the afternoon battle.

This was a "kill or be killed" contest.

Wearing colorful body armor, the gladiators marched

around the perimeter of the battlefield. They raised their weapons of choice — war chain, three-pronged trident spear, dagger, net, or lasso — to the cheers of the throng. After completing this customary display of strength, the gladiators stopped and stood in the presence of the emperor.

As innumerable warriors before them had done, these combatants shouted, *Ave, Caesar, morituri te salutant!* — "Hail, Caesar, those about to die salute thee!" Here's what happened next, according to *Fox's Book of Martyrs*:

> The combats now began again; the gladiators with nets tried to entangle those with swords, and when they succeeded mercilessly stabbed their antagonists to death with the three-pronged spear. When a gladiator had wounded his adversary, and had him lying helpless at his feet, he looked up at the eager faces of the spectators, and cried out, *Hoc habet!* "He has it!" and awaited the pleasure of the audience to kill or spare.[2]

Pause here for a moment. If you're like me, you may read this bit of history with a degree of disbelief. Did tens of thousands of people actually entertain themselves for an afternoon watching humans slaughter humans? Well, not only did this happen, but notice how the crowd reacted if a wounded warrior was hesitant to die. John Fox writes, "If the fatal signal of 'thumbs down' was given, the conquered was to be slain; and if he showed any reluctance to present his neck for the death blow, there was a scornful shout from the galleries, *Récipe ferrum!* "Receive the steel!"[3]

This particular day, Telemachus, a monk who journeyed from the countryside to encourage the churches in Rome, caught wind of the fights. Unfamiliar with such things, Telemachus went to the coliseum. What he witnessed broke his heart.

Stunned by the display of barbarism that many jaded souls had accepted as the status quo, motivated by his love for life and the knowledge that all people are made in the image of God, Telemachus did the unthinkable: He jumped from the stands onto the field and placed himself between two gladiators.

Clad only in a hermit's robe, armed only with a passion for God, Telemachus challenged the gladiators to cease their shedding of blood and the taking of life. The crowd and the gladiators were so enraged by his meddling in their "games" that Telemachus was slain on the spot — and then pelted with stones hurled by the audience.

History records that Telemachus's death wasn't in vain. There was something about witnessing the murder of this holy man that sent shock waves through the coliseum. God used the zeal and courage of one man to change the course of history. How? The Romans abandoned their gladiator games from that day forward.

This Is the Mark of a Christian

Nearly four hundred years before Telemachus sacrificed his life for the sake of others, another man stood before an individual of great influence and power. As the mobs grew restless and angrier by the minute, Jesus of Nazareth stood before Pontius Pilate, the fifth Prefect of the Roman province of Judea.

> Then the Jewish leaders took Jesus from Caiaphas to
> the palace of the Roman governor ... So Pilate came out

to them [the Jewish leaders] and asked, "What charges are you bringing against this man?"

"If he were not a criminal," they replied, "we would not have handed him over to you."

Pilate said, "Take him yourselves and judge him by your own law."

"But we have no right to execute anyone," they objected ...

Pilate then went back inside the palace, summoned Jesus and asked him, "Are you the king of the Jews?"

"Is that your own idea," Jesus asked, "or did others talk to you about me?"

"Am I a Jew?" Pilate replied. "Your own people and chief priests handed you over to me. What is it you have done?"

Jesus said, "My kingdom is not of this world. If it were, my servants would fight to prevent my arrest by the Jewish leaders. But now my kingdom is from another place."

"You are a king, then!" said Pilate.

Jesus answered, "You say that I am a king. In fact, the reason I was born and came into the world is to testify to the truth. Everyone on the side of truth listens to me."

"What is truth?" retorted Pilate.

JOHN 18:28-38

With the mobs demanding Jesus' crucifixion, Pilate handed Jesus over to die.

The scene inside Pilate's court is breathtaking and instructive. The power of Jesus is fully there — fully authentic. He doesn't argue with Pilate. He speaks truth and confidently lays down His life.

The distinguishing mark of a Christian, said the famed British preacher Charles Spurgeon, is their confidence in Christ's love for them and the offering of their love to Christ.[4] Because Jesus Christ has conquered sin, it's not up to us to conquer but instead to live in such a way that those within our sphere of influence know that Jesus Christ not only loves us but that He loves them too.

5

Taking the Long View *of Life*

The world and its desires pass away, but whoever
does the will of God lives forever.

1 JOHN 2:17

WHEN I FIRST MET CHUCK COLSON, THE LATE FOUNDER OF Prison Fellowship, I was in my thirties and serving in a different role for Focus on the Family. Back then, we had little interaction, but as the Lord began to entrust me with more responsibility, our paths crossed more often. Instead of just listening to Chuck, I was now visiting with this great giant of the faith. Over the years, I would share my heart and even my insecurities with Chuck. In response, he gave me his ear, and a special relationship blossomed. He gave me great advice on matters big and small.

Of the numerous admirable attributes Chuck possessed, his humility and long-term perspective about life stood out above the rest. He was always ready to share openly about his own faults and besetting sins. It takes a humble and broken man to openly admit that his own pride and out-of-control ego led to his downfall and to his label as a disgraced former member of the Nixon administration and a convicted felon, at that. I think the main reason his life was an open book was because he lived with an eternal, not a temporal, perspective. He saw every earthly "victory" as temporary. Very little, if anything, seemed to rattle him. Emotionally, he was never too high — or too low. He was an even-keeled man who lived life with an unruffled spirit of confidence.

I remember visiting with him during a trip to Naples, Florida, in spring 2008. There was a growing spirit of consternation over who would emerge as the Republican nominee for president. Some people said they would never vote for certain candidates for all kinds of reasons and sit out the election in protest. In addition, great angst over the rising candidacy of then-senator Barack Obama was evident. Strong opinions were being shared from all sides at the event we were attending, and Chuck patiently and intently listened to all of them, his arms folded. Finally somebody asked, "What do you think, Chuck?"

"What we do flows from who we are," he told the group, "so we should always vote our conscience. But we have to remember that politics is not perfect. We do not compromise our principles, but we often must nevertheless compromise. What is the greater good? Who more closely represents our values? That is the question."

That such a measured response would come from an individual considered by many to be President Nixon's hatchet man speaks to the wisdom of having an eternal and not a temporal perspective. Even though Colson disagreed with the vast majority of President Obama's agenda, Obama's election in 2008 did not rattle Chuck because he knew that the true treasure of this life — and the next — is secure (Matthew 6:19–20).

Just prior to his death on April 21, 2012, Chuck was talking about his philosophy of cultural engagement, and I'll never forget his response to a remark suggesting that Christians should be offended and fight fire with fire when ridiculed by "the other side" for their beliefs: "If a blind man steps on your foot, would you be mad and hold it against him?"

Chuck was always adept at putting circumstances in perspective. He was a wise man. He refused to play the hype game and declare that the sky was falling and that all hope was lost if an election should turn out a certain way.

"The greatest friend of truth is time," he once said, adding that "her greatest enemy is prejudice, and her constant companion, humility."

The Lesson of Mother Teresa

I've always been fascinated by the story of Mother Teresa, a humble Albanian nun who established the Missionaries of Charity order in India. She was born Agnes Bojaxhiu but took the name Teresa upon entering the Loreto Abbey in Ireland. The organization she founded ministered to orphans, the poor, and outcasts, as well as to the sick and dying. For years she was known and admired by those within her small sphere of influence, but otherwise an unknown figure to the rest of the world. That all changed when she agreed to sit down for a half-hour conversation with a British broadcaster named Malcolm Muggeridge.

It was Mother Teresa's first-ever television appearance. Muggeridge wasn't much impressed with the diminutive lady. He was also a bit frustrated by her refusal to follow his line of questioning. She wasn't giving him what he thought the conversation needed or what he speculated the audience wanted. The BBC reporter wanted her to talk about points of doctrine, but she was more interested in discussing the specifics of her work. Her responses were respectful but somewhat blunt and clearly not concerned about impressing anyone.

It's safe to say that Mother Teresa underwhelmed Muggeridge. It's not that he was unimpressed with her work but that she was content to quietly toil away in virtual anonymity. She wasn't interested in making headlines but rather trying to meet practical needs. When the show aired two months later in May 1968, the response shocked not only Muggeridge but also BBC executives. Viewers flooded the station with donations designated for the Missionaries of Charity. The public demanded that the interview be re-aired, which it was, and another wave of donations followed.

Muggeridge proposed an extensive documentary as a follow-up, and Mother Teresa reluctantly agreed, but only because she believed it would serve as a positive witness for Christ. Accompanied by a cameraman and producer, Muggeridge went to Calcutta to film the documentary. As he watched Mother Teresa out among the sick and the poor, he asked her how long she had been doing this, and he was shocked to learn she had been toiling in Calcutta's streets for nearly eighteen years. "It is my privilege to be here," she told him. "These are my people. These are the ones my Lord has given me to love."

"Do you ever get tired?" he asked. "Do you ever feel like quitting and letting someone else take over your ministry? After all, you are beginning to get older."

"Oh, no," she answered, "this is where the Lord wants me,

and this is where I am happy to be. I feel young when I am here. The Lord is so good to me. How privileged I am to serve Him."[1]

Muggeridge's documentary *Something Beautiful for God* was broadcast in late 1969 at the height of the cultural revolution in America, and once again the public enthusiastically embraced Mother Teresa and the work she was doing.

Why? What common denominator helped unify a wildly diverse body of viewers? Why were people who weren't even interested in matters of faith, let alone Christianity, so moved by Teresa's story that they requested to see it again and again?

I believe it was Mother Teresa's love for the gospel that made her attractive to a world that was hungry for truth and authenticity. It has struck me that people are drawn, almost intuitively, to the good and to that which lasts and to the person who does the will of God. Looking back on the phenomenon, Muggeridge reflected on the reason:

> Discussions are endlessly taking place about how to use a mass medium like television for Christian purposes, and all manner of devices are tried, from dialogues with learned atheists and humanists to pop versions of the psalms and psychedelic romps. Here was the answer. Just get on the screen a face shining and overflowing with Christian love; someone for whom the world is nothing and the service of Christ everything ... It doesn't matter how the face is lighted or shot; whether in front or profile, close-up or two-shot or long-shot; what questions are put, or by whom. The message comes over ... It might seem surprising, on the face of it, that an obscure nun of Albanian origins, very nervous — as was clearly apparent — in

front of the camera, somewhat halting in speech, should reach English viewers as no professional Christian apologist, bishop or archbishop, moderator or knockabout progressive dog-collared demonstrator ever has. But this is exactly what happened.[2]

The Gospel Is Nonpartisan

When the apostle Paul wrote his famous letter to the church at Rome, he did not categorize people into ideological or political camps. Instead, he identified the main problem that affects all people, namely, sin.

> I do not understand what I do. For what I want to do I do not do, but what I hate I do.
>
> ROMANS 7:15

Paul was speaking, of course, of the sinful human condition. Saint Augustine, known as the "doctor of the church," helped new believers understand this struggle even more vividly when he coined the phrase, *Incurvatus in se*, which literally means, "to curve inward on oneself." In many ways, this is exactly what sin is — an obsession with our own interests and concerns, not with others' needs and desires of the heart. In other words, everything becomes about me — from being right to being liked to being respected and admired — and especially to winning every argument or fight.

Sometimes we might do what's right — but for the wrong (usually selfish) reason. I am reminded of the story of the philosopher Diogenes. He was once seen sitting on a curb eating lentils and bread, a meager meal. A fellow philosopher, Aristippus, a man who lived well because he flattered the king, approached him and mocked his circumstance. "If you would learn to be subservient to the king," he snarled, "you would not have to live on lentils." Diogenes looked up with a smile, tilted his head, and replied, "Learn to live on lentils, and you will not have to cultivate the king."[3]

Developing a Humble Heart

Blaise Pascal once stated, "There are only two kinds of men: the righteous who think they are sinners and the sinners who think they are righteous."[4] C. S. Lewis agreed. "When a man is getting better," he once wrote, "he understands more and more clearly the evil that is still left in him. When a man is getting worse, he understands his own badness less and less. A moderately bad man knows he's not very good: a thoroughly bad man thinks he's all right."[5]

When it comes to the challenge of maintaining perspective, has it ever occurred to us that at the heart of almost every problem is the failure to recognize this fact of our faith? When we trust more in our own strength and power than His, our priorities are inevitably reordered, and not for the better. In our brashness we wind up taking God's seat and declaring ourselves both judge and jury. Indeed, almost all human misery is derived from not knowing who we are — and forgetting the One in whom we must place our trust and life.

"The meek man," wrote A. W. Tozer, "is not a human mouse afflicted with a sense of his own inferiority. Rather he may be in his moral life as bold as a lion and as strong as Samson; but he has stopped being fooled about himself. He has accepted God's estimate of his own life."[6]

When I consider the times I struggle the most with balancing what I see as my calling with what others expect and think of me, I'm comforted by the lessons found in Scripture. While numerous other moments and conversations in Jesus' ministry continued to juxtapose the clash of public expectation and sacred intention, perhaps nothing reveals it more dramatically than the momentousness of Palm Sunday, Good Friday, and Resurrection Day. As religious leaders and ordinary citizens wrestled with Jesus' claim to be the long-awaited Messiah, they often heard what they wanted to hear and not what Jesus was telling them.

We see this in the apostle John's record of how they treated Jesus during the Festival of the Tabernacles, a religious observance commemorating the time the children of Israel lived in temporary tents in the wilderness (John 7:1 – 44). Stretched over a week of events, the festivities included reenacting this encampment as Jewish people built tents and temporary "booths" to live in during the festival. Along with thousands of others, Jesus returned to Jerusalem for this major celebration, and He impressed the huge crowds gathered there for the holiday. He clearly had command of the Scriptures in a way that could best any rabbi or priest. He exhibited such authority and power alongside a gentleness and compassion that combined to make Him the most dynamic teacher who has ever lived.

As Jesus became more direct in revealing His identity as the Messiah, the public's expectations for Him to emerge as a political general increased to the point that they wanted to rally behind Him and show their support for what they concluded must be His anti-Roman cause. Thus, when Jesus entered the city for the Passover Festival, the crowds cheered with a rousing, "Hosanna!" (John 12:13) — a political battle cry essentially meaning, "Free us, O God! Save us from the Romans!" The people waved palm branches and laid down their cloaks to create a kind of royal red carpet for the man who claimed to be the Messiah and therefore would be seeking to restore their freedom. The palm branch had long been a symbol of victory and national triumph, dating back to the time Israel left Egypt (Leviticus 23:40). A contemporary parallel in our country would be a political rally for a charismatic candidate, complete with flag waving and red, white, and blue banners.

Jesus conveyed a different message about the kind of Savior He would be — a spiritual one and not a military one — by riding a young donkey in a gesture of humility and peace. While they expected the Messiah to ride a white steed or wave to the crowds from a chariot, the onlookers may have found Jesus' humility charming, sort of like a victorious general refusing the crown being offered. Seeing their response and the enthusiastic political fervor, Jesus is heartbroken. Luke writes, "As he approached Jerusalem and saw the city, he wept over it and said, 'If you, even you, had only known on this day what would bring you peace — but now it is hidden from your eyes'" (Luke 19:41 – 42).

Bible teacher and expert on Jewish history and culture Ray Vander Laan writes, "It seems that Jesus was saddened because His fellow Jews looked for military solutions to their problems rather than spiritual ones — to a political messiah rather than the Lamb of God."[7] Vander Laan describes the Jewish tradition of lamb selection day in which an unblemished young sheep would be chosen for offering sacrificially in the temple as part of the Passover Festival. The day that Jesus rode into town was lamb selection day, and the north temple gate through which He entered was known as the Sheep Gate, since it was used to bring the daily sacrifice to God's house. Jesus was symbolically very clear, but the Jewish people were so intent on reinforcing their own beliefs and expectations that they neither saw nor heard His message. He came as the ultimate sacrificial Lamb to bring peace, healing, and restoration to God's people for all time.[8] He did not come to camp in the desert and plan an attack on the Romans.

Could it be that we've lost sight of the Prince of Peace weeping over the misunderstanding of shortsighted followers? Could it be that we're called to reexamine our attitudes and refocus our sights on how best to serve God and reflect His character?

Even though He is addressing the Pharisees of His day, Jesus' description of how we hear His voice and follow Him is as relevant for us today:

> Very truly I tell you Pharisees, anyone who does not enter the sheep pen by the gate, but climbs in by some other way, is a thief and a robber. The one who enters by the gate is the shepherd of the sheep. The gatekeeper opens the gate for him, and the sheep listen to his voice. He calls his own sheep by name and leads them out. When he has brought out all his own, he goes on ahead of them, and his sheep follow him because they know his voice.
>
> JOHN 10:1–4

Anything that pulls us away from loving God and others

and from serving those around us and thereby reflecting God's heart and the example of Jesus must be considered troubling at best and idolatrous at worst. We need to work vigorously to carry out a healthy and strong engagement in the culture while avoiding attitudes and behaviors that undermine our Christian witness.

In late 1951, C. S. Lewis received a letter from British Prime Minister Winston Churchill, inviting him to receive the honorary title of Commander of the British Empire, a prestigious class in the Most Excellent Order of the British Empire. The honorees are recognized for their "gallantry and service" and lauded by the British people. It was, of course, a remarkable honor, but Lewis politely declined. Why? In a letter to the prime minister's secretary, Lewis wrote, "I feel greatly obliged to the Prime Minister, and so far as my personal feelings are concerned this honour would be highly agreeable." However, he added that many people said or believed that Christianity is basically "covert anti-Leftist propaganda, and my appearance in the Honours List would of course strengthen their hands. It is therefore better that I should not appear there."[9]

Despite the prestige attached to the honor, Lewis was inclined to see the bigger picture and selflessly decline. I wonder how many of us would do likewise if offered a similar decoration whose awarding might cause nonbelievers to stay away from what we passionately believe to be true. Our faith demands that we look at things through the long lens. In the end, we know the final score. Our joy is not dependent on circumstance or earthly honors. Our significance is rooted not in institutions or mere mortals but in the promise and assurance of Christ's return.

My prayer is that we will return to the essence of who Jesus is and model our choices, behaviors, and speech on His actions during His time on earth. My hope is that we will listen for the voice of our Shepherd and follow accordingly. We remain engaged and care deeply about our culture because it is comprised of people made in God's image. But we cannot lose sight of our ultimate purpose — to live lives that glorify God. We live in a wonderful country and have been richly blessed. If you woke up to a new day today, I have good news for you: God has a plan and purpose for you. Grumbling and mumbling our way through tough times will get us nowhere.

Always Be Ready!

Live such good lives among the pagans that, though they accuse you of doing wrong, they may see your good deeds and glorify God on the day he visits us.

1 PETER 2:12

DRIVING IS A METAPHOR FOR LIFE. YOU HAVE YOUR LEFT-lane or fast-lane drivers who tend to be quite intense and are always in a hurry to get from point A to point B. Then you have your middle-of-the-road motorists who take everything in moderation. Finally you have your right-lane or slow-lane folks who meet every emergency leisurely.

Into which camp do you fall?

I hate to admit it, but for years I was squarely in the fast-lane camp, both literally and figuratively. Aggressive action is sometimes required, of course, but my temper and sense of justice have gotten me in trouble on the road all too often. Even after years as a Christian, I would grow incredibly irritated with bad drivers. In retrospect, it was quite ridiculous. My temper would rage if somebody cut me off or I perceived they were driving too slowly and impeding my progress. I once chased a driver who had especially offended me. What a fool I was! The incident didn't escalate beyond a brief conversation, but what if it had? We've all read stories about violent road rage that ends with a bullet through a window. I'm embarrassed to look back on that season of my life. Thankfully, the Lord took me to task over this arrogant behavior, and not a minute too soon. I was behaving badly, and in doing so, I was serving as a terrible Christian witness. Here I was working for an evangelical organization and acting like a spoiled brat.

Another time, a colleague and I stopped at an Avis Rental Car counter one afternoon while traveling for our ministry. It was a scene straight out of *Seinfeld* as the clerk explained how they had received the reservation but somehow failed to hold it. In response, my traveling companion, under whose name the reservation was held, went ballistic on this poor clerk. While no profanity was uttered, the conversation was disrespectful. The Avis representative handled the heat masterfully and promised to investigate. After a minute, he said, "Oh, you work for Focus on the Family. I love that ministry!" In an instant, my colleague's attitude changed, and he turned supersweet as he thanked the agent for listening to our radio broadcast. I felt like slinking off into the corner.

What hypocrites we can be while living out our Christian faith! We profess to believe principles we don't personally possess. It's as though we are double-minded — which we all too often are. The apostle Paul, in a moment of great vulnerability, wrote, "I do not understand what I do. For what I want to do I do not do, but what I hate I do" (Romans 7:15). We may find comfort in knowing that one of the pillars of the church was at times a hypocrite. But this doesn't let us off the hook. Like Paul, we must constantly work and pray toward spiritual transformation. I try to regularly ask myself, if my behavior were evaluated in an ecclesiastical court of law, would I be found guilty of being a Christian? Or would I be charged with impersonating a person of faith?

There is no room within Christianity for arrogance or smugness, and all of us must be careful to seek the high moral ground when it comes to our pursuit of humility. Tim Keller warns us:

> The teaching seems simple and obvious. The problem is that it takes great humility to understand humility, and even more to resist the pride that comes so naturally with even a discussion of the subject.
>
> We are on slippery ground because humility cannot be attained directly. Once we become aware of the poison of pride, we begin to notice it all around us. We hear it in the sarcastic, snarky voices in newspaper columns and weblogs. We see it in civic, cultural, and business leaders who never admit weakness or failure. We see it in our neighbors and some friends with their jealousy, self-pity, and boasting.
>
> And so we vow not to talk or act like that. If we then notice "a humble turn of mind" in ourselves, we immediately become smug — but that is pride in our humility. If we catch ourselves doing *that* we will be particularly impressed with how nuanced and subtle we have become. Humility is so shy. If you begin talking about it, it leaves. To even ask the question, "Am I humble?" is to not be so. Examining your own heart, even for pride, often leads to being proud about your diligence and circumspection.[1]

It's easy to sit in judgment of a fellow sister or brother,

especially from afar. When I was tapped to lead Focus on the Family in 2005, a *Wall Street Journal* reporter talked with me about my new role. She wanted to know my perspective on the state of the pro-life effort, and I said something I later came to regret. Although I was quick to affirm our continued commitment to protecting the sanctity of life, I suggested that after thirty-plus years of engagement, the movement didn't have much to show for the effort. The comment came out of my frustration over the continued killing of children at the tragic and horrific rate of approximately one million per year. After four decades, *Roe v. Wade* remains the law of the land, and that fact greatly disappoints me. Alas, if the gauge of the success of the pro-life movement is the reversal of *Roe*, my comments would have been accurate. The reality, of course, is that *much good has been achieved* in the battle for life. In fact, in the court of public opinion, life is winning, and by a significant margin. Technology has confirmed what we all know to be true — that a baby is not a blob of tissue but a developing person, sustainable within the first trimester. You can see the dimensions and the amazing detail of life thanks to the wonders of ultrasound technology. In fact, this technology more than anything else is confirming that the pre-born child really is a human being, and people are concluding that abortion is not something a civilized culture should practice.

My comments to the *Wall Street Journal* reporter were a bit hasty, and I can't deny that pride was a factor in my reflection. I was acting like the left-lane driver stuck behind a slow-poke. I was being impatient and imprudent. Instead of considering the history and the contributions of the movement, I had concluded that I had found a better way forward.

I've always had a competitive and straightforward personality. So when a challenge is posed, I'm inclined to meet it head-on and in the quickest, most efficient manner possible. I often approach public policy matters, including key issues such as abortion and marriage, with this perspective. If five people on the Supreme Court won't acknowledge that a pre-born baby deserves life, let's keep pushing them, I say, but at the same time let's figure out a way to save as many of those million children dying each year as we can. Some people disagreed, judging it foolish to talk with "the other side" of the abortion divide. I respect their opinion but simply disagree. For me, this is a "Schindler's list" moment. Nevertheless, my comments decrying a lack of progress were impertinent and inaccurate. In my quest for more progress, I had failed to acknowledge the legions of pro-life stalwarts who are doing great things to protect the most defenseless among us.

Christian Humility Is Not Thinking Less of Yourself; It Is Thinking of Yourself Less

Within Christian circles, Max Lucado is a household name, beloved for his gentle and inspiring books. The San Antonio–based pastor is a publishing icon. More than twenty million of his titles are in circulation, and his throngs of readers eagerly await each year's new release. Now at about this point you'd probably expect me to share a story of Lucado's humility, to tell you that even with his bestseller status, he doesn't struggle with pride or ego. But the fact is, he does, which is why Lucado is winning the battle *we all fight*, one way or the other.

Looking back to his early writing days he reflects: "I really think God said, 'I can't trust Lucado with too much, but I'm going to give him this ability and see how he handles it ... OK, he didn't mess that up. OK, here's another idea,'" he says. "I try to be faithful. I try to get my manuscripts in on time. I try not to let it go to my head, but sometimes I think too highly of myself."[2]

As minister of preaching to a congregation of three thousand, Lucado is refreshingly candid when he discusses the battle he endures with his ego. "I confessed it to the church," he stated. "I was sick of always wanting to know if our church was as big as the others. A man gave me some great advice. He reminded me that when another church does well, we all do well. After he said that, I suddenly saw Oak Hills as one tiny corpuscle in the body of Christ." And despite having sold millions of books, he acknowledges he always hopes to sell more. "I take too much pride in that. I ideally want to be able to say that I can be content if 500 people read my books rather than 500,000. But I can't ... I know competitiveness can be healthy and good, unless it is pride driven. It's a struggle for me."[3]

Max Lucado's candidness should serve as a good model, and though most of us are not faced with balancing our gifts with widespread fame and even fortune, the premise is instructive. It's easy to justify our own out-of-control pride and ego. Lucado could easily suggest he's interested in selling more books because he wants to reach more souls for the Lord. But he knows better — and he's honest about it! A person obsessed with their physical image may claim they're simply concerned with good grooming. A workaholic tells their spouse they're providing for the family, but the truth is, they're finding their identity at the workplace, not in the person and divinity of Jesus. On and on it goes.

Of pride and its pull, Puritan writer William Jenkyn puts it well. "It is only a Christian of strong grace," he said, "that can bear the strong wine of his commendations without the spiritual intoxication of pride."[4]

The gospel tells us that our acceptance is not based on our performance (our works); instead it is a gift freely given, without strings attached. This is what we call grace. Only when we fully embrace this gift of grace do we stop trying to win the small battles and promote ourselves in the process. Otherwise, life becomes about the victory, which eventually leads to us becoming the predator and the world our prey.

Judge Not, That You Be Not Judged

I regret not having had the pleasure of meeting the late Francis Schaeffer, an articulate and enthusiastic Christian apologist perhaps best known for his book titled *A Christian Manifesto*.[5] Dr. Schaeffer was brave and bold. In joining the fight to protect the unborn innocents, he challenged the liberal theologians of his day — those who suggested that man, not God, was the measure of all things. One of his lesser-known books, *Death in the City*, contains a remarkably instructive passage on pride and humility.

To open the discussion, Schaeffer references the second chapter of Paul's letter to the church at Rome:

> Do you, my friend, pass judgment on others? You have no excuse at all, whoever you are. For when you judge others,

and then do the same things which they do, you condemn
yourself. We know that God is right when he judges the
people who do such things as these. But you, my friend,
do those very things yourself for which you pass judgment
on others! Do you think you will escape God's judgment?

ROMANS 2:1–3 GNT

Pivoting off Paul's inspired instruction, Schaeffer proceeds
to present a hypothetical and provocative scenario. Just imagine, he suggested, that every person is born into the world with
an invisible tape recorder (this was written in 1969) around
their neck. However, the tapes will only turn on when negative
moral judgments are made by the wearer such as "He's so lazy"
or "She's such a gossip." This process of conditional periodic
recording will continue for the duration of the person's life.

Schaeffer now shifts the scene. Those who had been wearing the recorders now find themselves standing before God.
According to the telling, many in the crowd are pleading for
immunity, claiming they were never even introduced to the
person of Christ. "Very well," God thunders. "Since you claim
not to know My laws, I will set aside My perfect standard of
righteousness. Instead I will judge you on this." He then proceeds to push the button on the recorder, and together they
listen as the individual's own voice pours forth a stream of
condemnation.

God declares, "This will be the basis of My judgment: how
well have you kept the moral standards you proved that you
understood by constantly applying them to those around you.
Here you accused someone of lying, yet have you ever stretched
the truth? You were angry at that fellow for being selfish, yet

have you ever put your own interests above someone else's needs?"

Schaeffer concluded, "And every person will be silent. For no one has consistently lived up to the standard he demands of others."[6] Do you find this as convicting as I do?

Strive for Peace with Everyone

The ongoing challenge for Christians in an ever-changing culture is this: How do we express a Christian ethos in a way that draws people into the discussion? How can we always be ready to serve as a witness to the love of Jesus? We are believers called by Jesus Christ to spread His good news. While we cannot compromise our principles and doctrine, we also must be compassionate and considerate and not expect the people of the world to act like Christians. By the same token, we don't want to start acting like those who live according to the principles of this world. It requires a delicate and thoughtful approach to life. A pastor I know recently posed this provocative question to his congregation: when engaging the culture, "Are we making a point or making a difference?"[7] In other words, are we obsessed with being right to the exclusion of living the gospel?

We are living in an increasingly bifurcated culture. At the same time an appreciation for orthodox Christianity is growing in some sectors, agnosticism and intolerance for Christian belief are on the rise too. Thus, navigating the rocky landscape is proving difficult, especially since many of us are easily offended. When we're puffed up with pride, we tend to take any difference of opinion personally. I was initially offended when the criticism began to roll in over my comments that the pro-life movement had been ineffectual. I should have been grateful that people were willing to help me see what I was missing.

When it comes to repelling the destructive nature of pride, the very best news is that the closer we grow to the Lord, the further away from pride we will be. That's because, as C. S. Lewis reminds us:

> In God, you come up against the something which is in every respect immeasurably superior to yourself. Unless you know God as that — and, therefore, know yourself as nothing in comparison — you do not know God at all. As long as you are proud you cannot know God. A proud man is always looking down on things and people: and, of course, as long as you are looking down, you cannot see something that is above you.[8]

I learned my lesson the hard way. Instead of looking up at the giants of the pro-life movement, instead of taking into consideration all the ways the Lord has used them to save babies' lives over the years, I was arrogant, assuming I knew a better way.

Are you living in a constant state of readiness as a Christian? If you stood trial, accused of being a believer, would there be sufficient evidence in your behavior to substantiate the claim? Every interaction we have with another person either enhances or diminishes a person's openness to God.

No One *Is Beyond* the Reach of God

The law was brought in so that the trespass might increase. But where sin increased, grace increased all the more.

ROMANS 5:20

The Reverend Graham J. Baird is the senior pastor of First Presbyterian Church in Colorado Springs. Prior to coming to Colorado, Graham served as the founding pastor of Highlands Church in Paso Robles, California. The ministry started with twenty-five people in a drive-in movie theater and has since grown to over two thousand weekly attenders. Graham's philosophy has been to pull down the barriers and make it easier for those wanting to come to church to learn about God. He has done a good job. Wherever he's been a pastor, whether in rural California or the front range of the Rocky Mountains, he has led with a straightforward ministerial motto: "No perfect people allowed" — pastor included.

During his time in Paso Robles, Graham encountered a variety of family scenarios, including a lesbian couple married in a state where same-sex marriage was legal. They began coming to his church and eventually had twins via in vitro fertilization. He had an opportunity to lovingly share the Bible's perspective on human sexuality. They continued to attend. When the couple asked to have their children baptized, he had a dilemma on his hands. According to his Reformed theology, the baptism of a child does not "save" a person but represents a commitment from the Christian parent to raise the child — or children — in the faith. Graham explained that given the couple's same-sex relationship, he couldn't ask them to present the child and make that commitment since they weren't actually members of the church. They were disappointed. Graham asked why they didn't simply find a church that would accommodate their request. Their response was powerful. "This is the only church where we have felt loved in," they told him. The children were later presented for baptism by their grandparents, who were members of the church.

Graham went on to explain what I believe strongly — that people know very quickly whether or not they are loved. The fact that this couple continued to attend — even though the church's theology with regard to sexuality was at odds with their personal actions — suggests that Highlands Church truly loved them for a variety of reasons, but especially for this one: They know that nobody is beyond the reach of God.

Taking Inventory

When it comes to loving those with whom we disagree on any number of issues — especially issues that have to do with our faith — I sometimes wonder if we really believe what we say we believe and what the Bible professes to be true — that God loves our "enemies" just as much as He loves you and me. In my quiet time and Bible reading, I'm continuously reminded that Jesus was not ashamed to be seen with adulterers, prostitutes, and tax collectors. But even more shocking and telling is this: He didn't just seek these people out; many sought Him. He drew sinners to His side. Why? How? Some suggest it was because of His charismatic and magnetic personality. Others point to His divinity and supernatural spirit. I agree with these reasons. I believe He attracted crowds because He had a firm, loving, and gracious nature. And I also believe He drew people to His side because they could sense that He truly and deeply loved them — despite all of their imperfections. In my role at Focus on the Family, I've felt convicted to do what I can do to break down the barriers in my little corner of the kingdom. This is why I've engaged homosexual activists and even abortion providers in conversations. I want to get to know them. I want to listen to them and hear the pain in their hearts.

Oh, I know the cynics will say it's a waste of time. Why cast pearls before swine? I do realize there's a need to show discretion and be wise about our interactions with others, especially when associations can be misinterpreted and even possibly used to damage our Christian witness. But I believe these incidents are few and far between. All too often we're reluctant to meet with the opposition because we're sure that people will get the wrong impression about us. In other words, we're more concerned about protecting our reputation than about boldly sharing the love of Jesus with them. There are other reasons, none of which are very compelling. I once knew a Christian who refused to meet with the opposition because he was afraid he'd begin liking them; in his mind, establishing friendships would compromise his ability to publicly criticize them.

Trying to Practice What We Preach

Colorado Springs has an alternative weekly newspaper called the *Independent*. The largest privately owned publication in the state, it offers an eclectic assortment of stories, most of them from a progressive editorial slant. For many years, the *Indy* has either ignored Focus or criticized it, even mocking the ministry, mostly for its conservative approach to family and social issues. In fact, one week's issue featured an exaggerated and unflattering cartoonish depiction of our founder, Dr. James Dobson, on its cover. Reporters and columnists have regularly poked fun at us. The relationship between their publisher, John Weiss, and his team and Focus has been icy for years, and if there was any exchange between us, it was purely perfunctory.

This chronic tension disappointed me, if for no other reason than it contradicted the teachings of Scripture. When the apostle Paul wrote that "our struggle is not against flesh and blood, but against the rulers, against the authorities, against the powers of this dark world and against the spiritual forces of evil in the heavenly realms" (Ephesians 6:12), he was trying to help us put earthly relationships into proper perspective. Our enemy is not someone with whom we disagree ideologically or even theologically. Yet so often this is exactly how we treat them. How we communicate our animosity varies — through rancorous argument, deliberate stone-cold silence, or somewhere in between. Avoiding others or taking subtle potshots may appear to be a more civil approach to disagreements, but we're called to *engage* the world, not ignore it.

Without sounding too myopic or Pollyannaish, I would say that a Christian's response to an oppositional perspective or person should greatly differ from the world's typical reaction. I've appreciated Fuller Theological Seminary's president Richard Mouw's insight on this topic. Sharing biblical truth in a secular world can be difficult, but it's always good and healthy to acknowledge the reality of passion and emotion when engaging differences of opinion. Dr. Mouw suggests putting ourselves in the other person's shoes. "For starters," he said, "concentrate on your own sinfulness and the other person's humanness."[1] Keep in mind how pointed and direct Paul's words to Titus were, urging believers "to slander no one, to be peaceable and considerate, and always to be gentle toward everyone" (Titus 3:2). Paul was no soft or apathetic warrior. He was, in fact, a paradoxical personality — gentle, yet firm; strong, yet compassionate.

There is a critical need for personal humility. Show me a person who constantly lashes out at an opponent, and there's a very good chance he or she is struggling mightily with an inflated ego and burgeoning pride.

I am committed to doing everything I can to ensure that my personal and our corporate interactions are respectful and grace filled — interactions that include everyone from friends inside President Obama's White House to reporters at our local independent newspaper. And how can we possibly behave any differently, especially when we recall Paul's words to the church at Colossae. "Be wise in the way you act toward outsiders," he wrote. "Make the most of every opportunity. Let your conversation be always full of grace, seasoned with salt, so that you may know how to answer everyone" (Colossians 4:5 – 6). As I think of our ongoing relationship with the *Indy*, I must ask: Are our interactions always full of grace? It's a tough question. I hope so.

Change often comes slowly and with difficulty, but the Lord

regularly provides us with opportunities to get it right. We simply have to pay attention and look for these invitations, which are often disguised as problems. I've welcomed the opportunity to sit down for coffee with John Weiss several times. Our visits have been not only enjoyable but also instructive. For example, each year, readers of the *Indy* are asked to rate everything from local pizza parlors to landscape and garden companies. Other categories are ideological or political in nature. In early 2011, Focus was mockingly awarded the "Claim to Shame Award" for, among other things, our continued support of traditional marriage and our ongoing advocacy to protect the sanctity of life. To be fair, we shared the award with a cantankerous local politician who, while holding his Bible during the opening prayer of the legislative session, once famously kicked a *Denver Post* cameraman.[2] Being presented this award was clearly a tongue-in-check, acrimonious gesture, but two of my associates decided to respond in Christian love and have some fun at the same time. I'm glad they did.

Gary Schneeberger is Focus on the Family's vice president of communications. A former journalist, Gary has great rapport with reporters. His colleague, Rajeev Shaw, is equally charismatic and engaging. Rajeev has been given the task of building relationships with local community organizations. These are two good guys with a strong commitment to the Lord and a passion for loving people. When we received notice of the award, Gary and Rajeev accepted the *Indy*'s invitation to attend their award banquet, an annual affair held at a local restaurant. *Indy* representatives were shocked. No recipient of the "Shame" award had ever bothered to respond, let alone attend the event! But Gary and Rajeev did, and in doing so, forged a unique friendship with my friend, *Indy*'s John Weiss. They didn't compromise any principles by attending; they simply treated John as a fellow traveler along this long road of life.

If this had been all that happened, it would have been enough — but there's more to the story. In the months following the conferring of the award, John Weiss and I began talking about our mutual passion for placing foster kids in forever families. He didn't agree with a lot of Focus's priorities, but when it came to the conviction that every child deserves a safe and loving home, John and I were on the same page. Weiss told a local reporter, "When I heard what they were doing with foster care, which is trying to support the families which are adopting the kids, giving them everything from a night out, without the kids … to cleaning to cooking, to just being cousins, saying 'We're going to help out.' We thought this was wonderful."[3] In response to this mutual conviction, we planned a local event together to raise community awareness of the three hundred – plus kids waiting to be placed with permanent families. It was a small meeting at a local college on a Saturday afternoon, but it was a good start and indicative of how Christians are called to engage culture. One curious family drove more than fifty miles to learn more about adopting out of the foster care system. Will they adopt? Only time will tell.

To be sure, John and I don't see eye-to-eye about foster care rules. John is in favor of allowing same-sex couples to adopt; I am not. I believe God designed every child to have a mother and a father, and to open the door to same-sex parenting inevitably deprives them of either a mother or a father. I'll continue to try to persuade him, and I suspect he'll try to work on me. Still, on this one weekend, we were able to find common ground for the sake of children in need. A comment from one of the *Indy*'s writers nicely summed up the essence and product of our relationship. "Focus and the *Indy* are just never going to agree on many things," she wrote. "But starting with our support of the ministry's foster care initiative, maybe there are ways we can work together to benefit the community. I mean, after all, my bonafide hippie mom always said it was 'wrong to judge people.'"[4]

We have indeed found more opportunities to partner with the *Indy* to better our shared community, none more public than a benefit concert we cosponsored on July 4, 2012, for victims of a wildfire that devastated Colorado Springs. The morning after the blaze destroyed 346 homes en route to consuming more than 18,000 acres of land, Gary Schneeberger called John Weiss and suggested we team up to raise money for the victims. A little more than a week later, thousands turned out for A Community Rises, a free event at the city's largest concert venue that featured performances by our city's philharmonic orchestra, Michael Martin Murphey, and Isaac Slade, lead singer of the multiple-Grammy-nominated band The Fray. Nearly $300,000 was raised in one night at the concert and via an unprecedented statewide live broadcast of the show on multiple television stations.

Asked by the media about our partnership with the *Indy* and other groups in our community that may not agree with our biblical views on social issues, Gary said, "At a time like this, everybody's ideology is the same. People who have been burned out of their homes need our help."[5]

Our neighbors may know we are Christians by our love, as the old song goes, but they will only know about the love of Jesus if we also share with them the truth about His life poured out as a sacrifice.

8

Don't Be a Miserable Christian

But thanks be to God that, though you used to be slaves to sin, you have come to obey from your heart the pattern of teaching that has now claimed your allegiance. You have been set free from sin and have become slaves to righteousness.

ROMANS 6:17–18

IF YOU ARE A CHRISTIAN, ARE YOU ENJOYING THE PEACE AND contentment that come with the assurance of eternal life? Would it be obvious in your countenance, in the way you engage with others and go about your day? If not, why not?

I've crossed paths with many unhappy Christians lately, and I suspect you have too. It's a peculiar thing to have received such an extraordinary gift and yet to grumble your way along life's road. The reasons for dissatisfaction are many and may well be temporary in nature. We will have, of course, the inevitable setback, such as losing a job or squabbling with a spouse. It's natural for our mood to sway based on circumstance. We're fallible and emotional creatures. What I'm getting at is the degree of our joy and general sense of contentment, given the faith we claim to possess.

Some time ago, my colleague Ken Windebank came up with a marvelous idea to create a special commercial for Focus on the Family to be aired during an NFL playoff game. It was just two days after then-Broncos quarterback Tim Tebow led his Denver team to an upset win over the Pittsburgh Steelers. The matchup between the Broncos and New England Patriots was looming, and Ken proposed running a spot featuring kids reciting one of the most famous Scriptures of all — John 3:16 (to see it, Google "John 3:16 ad"). Children were recruited and the filming took place over the course of an afternoon. In the midst of it all, a spontaneous thing occurred. A little girl named Channing, after hearing the verse recited, let out a big "Wow!" This caused me to wonder, *When was the last time I stood and stared in awe and wonder at the vastness of God's love and the magnificence of his salvation?*

I remember my early days of fatherhood when I would quietly slip into Trent's and Troy's rooms and watch their tiny chests rise and fall with every peaceful breath. It left me fumbling for words that never came. Not only was I nearly speechless at the beauty of the new life before me; I was humbled to be given the new name "Dad."

In those moonlit nights, David's words took on new meaning:

I praise you because I am fearfully and wonderfully made;
your works are wonderful,
I know that full well.

PSALM 139:14

So if the gift of new human life strikes with such a spirit of astonishment, how, then, does the promise of eternal life grab you? If you ask me, Channing's single word deftly and powerfully sums up the Christian response to the gospel: *Wow!*

How about your reaction to the gospel?

How's your sense of "Wow!" these days? In tough times, it's

easy to get deflated and buried in our own little story. We allow ourselves to be shaped and influenced by the very sin that Jesus came to save us from.

It's time to look up and "ponder anew what the Almighty can do," as the hymnist wrote. Is the search for awe difficult? Perhaps it's a matter of personal priorities. In his book *The Ragamuffin Gospel*, Brennan Manning quotes Rabbi Abraham Joshua Heschel: "Never once in my life did I ask God for success or wisdom or power or fame. I asked for wonder, and He gave it to me."[1] Have you asked for the same?

When was the last time you stopped to ponder in wonder and awe at the promise of life eternal for those who accept Jesus as Lord and Savior? Many years ago, George Beverly Shea, the longtime friend and colleague of Dr. Billy Graham, penned the great hymn "The Wonder of It All." It begins like this:

> There's the wonder of sunset at evening,
> The wonder as sunrise I see;
> But the wonder of wonders that thrills my soul
> Is the wonder that God loves me.

I once asked some folks how they maintain their sense of wonder and awe of the Almighty and the amazing gift of His Son. Here's what Stan wrote in response:

> *No matter how much the world goes through, with all of its sadness and destruction and horror, God's plan is working everything in service of an optimal plan, and will reconcile everything in the end! (Ephesians 1:8b – 11) Wow! In the face of everything discouraging in this world, God's promises provide the ultimate encouragement. He truly is worthy of glory!*

Stan is correct. The Lord is the Master Weaver who can even use unfortunate circumstances to further the spread of His kingdom on earth. To the same question, Ken offered this practical observation:

> God has maintained the sense of wonder for my wife and me by placing adoption on our hearts. We have three adopted kids, with a fourth on the way, and there isn't a day that we don't experience a sense of wonder and WOW. My two sons and I watched Superman tonight. As I was putting our five-year-old to bed, we were talking about the movie. He commented on how many things Superman could do. I told him that though it was a good movie, it was also make-believe. He thought about it for a few seconds and said, "I don't want to be Superman. I like being me." Words of wisdom to end the night with. We started this whole adoption process at a late stage in life, and although I am worn-out at the end of the day, I have never experienced so much joy and wonder. To think that God chose us to bring these kids "home." I am truly a blessed man.

I've always liked the poem by William Wordsworth titled "Character of the Happy Warrior." Though not so intended, it is an appropriate charge to Christians who seek God's strength in their efforts to engage the culture winsomely. Space does not permit me to share it in its entirety, but here are a few poignant verses:

> Who is the happy Warrior? Who is he
> That every man in arms should wish to be? …
> Whose high endeavours are an inward light
> That makes the path before him always bright …

Who, doomed to go in company with Pain,
And Fear, and Bloodshed, miserable train!
Turns his necessity to glorious gain ...
Finds comfort in himself and in his cause;
And, while the mortal mist is gathering, draws
His breath in confidence of Heaven's applause:
This is the happy Warrior; this is He
That every Man in arms should wish to be.[2]

As the leader of Focus on the Family, I've always seen my role as something akin to the happy warrior. My mood is generally upbeat and optimistic. Even when news reports are discouraging—a daily occurrence—I tend to be optimistic because, to borrow a line from the old Christian spiritual: "He's got the whole world in His hands." Indeed He does. As a result, I'm confident about tomorrow because I know the One in whose hands tomorrow rests.

In the context of how we manage the present and face the future as Christians, fear is the opposite of this supernatural spirit of confidence. It's quite easy to discover what and in whom we trust by examining what causes us anxiety and sleepless nights. Does a volatile stock market cause us to begin digging the bunker in the backyard? Wisdom dictates that we plan and get ready for the unexpected, and this will look different for different people. But if the love of God assures us of our eternal future, what else really matters?

The late Dr. D. Martyn-Lloyd Jones put it bluntly: "We should be much more concerned about the state of the Church herself than about the state of the world outside the Church. It seems increasingly evident that the explanation of the present state of Christendom is to be found inside the Church and not outside."[3]

It surprises me when many Christians engage in work to redeem the culture with a somber, morose, and even anxious spirit. I don't pretend to be smarter or more spiritually mature than anyone else, but this particular attitude is curious and even a bit contradictory. A dear friend of mine who is a pastor once preached on an uplifting text of Scripture. He spoke of God's sovereignty and perfect will, of His love and goodness and graciousness. He was not serving up weak tea; he preached about the centrality and sufficiency of the gospel, as well as the power and glory of God. After the service, a well-known evangelist who had been in attendance approached the minister. "You're giving them too much hope," he told him bluntly — and with that, he turned on his heels and walked out of the church.

In a recent conversation with a friend, he drew a parallel between a mutual acquaintance of ours and my childhood. The person in question is a real survivor who currently manages a rather chaotic existence. My friend said it reminded him of me and the untraditional life of my youth.

While I recognize the similarities, I suggested there was a significant distinction between the two. Unlike this friend of ours who appears content with his troubled lot, I managed to survive abandonment and loneliness for one main reason: I lived in a constant state of hope, always praying and dreaming that I would someday, someway, trade chaos for order and an unconventional family life for a traditional family. Having hope in a better future gave me a measure of strength to carry on, no matter how heavy the burdens.

Thomas Fuller once wrote, "Hope is the only tie which keeps the heart from breaking."[4] This is why the apostle Paul urged the Romans to "be joyful in hope, patient in affliction, faithful in prayer" (Romans 12:12). Hope in that which is noble can ease pain and bring comfort. Hope will help to keep despair and despondency at bay.

Turning to the First-Century Church for Perspective and Instruction

Lessons from the early church have always reminded me of the importance of rejoicing in the Lord always, despite the experience of difficult circumstances. People often forget that it wasn't easy to be a Christian in the first century. In fact, that's an understatement. Persecution was pervasive and endorsed by authorities. If someone was interested in winning a popularity contest, he or she didn't align with Christian theology or even socialize with the radicals who subscribed to its teachings. In many ways, baptism in the early church was akin to a suicide mission, especially since many who championed the faith eventually died a martyr's death. It seemed that the whole world stood in opposition to Paul and the early adherents of the faith. We read in the book of Acts that the Jewish leaders were offended by the message, as were those who worshiped at the temple to Artemis. Government officials objected to those who expressed allegiance to anyone but the state, especially since the emperor was considered to be divine and the true Lord.

An interesting passage in Acts details a firsthand critique of Paul's missionary work. We learn that citizens in Ephesus were concerned not just about the spiritual revolution that was afoot but about the economic impact of religious conversion as well:

> About that time there arose a great disturbance about the Way. A silversmith named Demetrius, who made silver shrines of Artemis, brought in a lot of business for the craftsmen there. He called them together, along with the workers in related trades, and said: "You know, my friends, that we receive a good income from this business. And you see and hear how this fellow Paul has convinced and led astray large numbers of people here in Ephesus and in practically the whole province of Asia. He says that gods made by human hands are no gods at all. There is danger not only that our trade will lose its good name, but also that the temple of the great goddess Artemis will be discredited; and the goddess herself, who is worshiped throughout the province of Asia and the world, will be robbed of her divine majesty."
>
> ACTS 19:23–27

At the time, the gospel was countercultural. It was not just a ceremony or isolated philosophy but also a force that penetrated every angle of life. This makes the zealousness of the early followers even more profound and inspiring. Paul's challenge to early believers was bold and direct and was clearly influenced by belief in the Old Testament understanding of God. Paul undoubtedly found his strength and assurance in any number of ancient texts.

PSALM 27:1: "The LORD is the stronghold of my life — of whom shall I be afraid?"

PSALM 46:1: "God is our refuge and strength, an ever-present help in trouble."

ZECHARIAH 4:6: " 'Not by might nor by power, but by my Spirit,' says the LORD Almighty."

The Gospel Is the Way by Which Christians Grow

Tim Keller of Redeemer Presbyterian Church is enjoying tremendous success in his New York City ministry. His church is defying national trends—in an undeniably liberal metropolitan area, no less. With nearly 70 percent of his congregation comprised of single persons and those under the age of forty, conventional wisdom suggests teaching that affirms orthodox Christian doctrine on such matters as marriage, sex, and abortion wouldn't be warmly embraced by large audiences. Yet, this is exactly what has happened for the last decade. Why?

Tim obviously has strong talents on many levels, and he is an especially gracious man who conducts himself with great humility. He is not just an intellectual, a theologian, and a bestselling author, but he is also a Christian gentleman. But it's more than mere manners that makes him effective. Tim has successfully identified the source of a Christian's strength and regularly puts it into words. He regularly reminds his church members that they don't have to perform—they don't have to "measure up" to the world's standards. Instead, they can rest in the assurance that comes from knowing God. Living with this type of assurance is exceptionally freeing. It constantly reminds us that there is no good reason to be miserable, to carry this great burden of believing that the fate of the entire world rests on your shoulders.

How it Affects Our Behavior

I have to be reminded about this too, especially in my role as the president of a large ministry. Like most other organizations, Focus on the Family has been feeling the effects of the economic malaise of the last few years. Our budget has been reduced by over $50 million since 2009, four years after becoming president. We have reduced the number of team members from a high of nearly 1,200 to 650. I've had days when I wonder what the Lord is up to, as I quietly ask Him if He wants me to be doing something else. Am I the problem? Time after time, I have sensed His presence urging me on, reminding me that it's my job to be faithful and to help manage the ministry. The Lord will take care of the finances. And wouldn't you know it — in the toughest of times I have learned the most valuable lessons! He doesn't want me to fret over the budget; He wants me to grow closer to His heart.

Tim Keller's audience at Redeemer Church finds itself in a somewhat similar place. Many of them have come to New York City in search of success and stardom. They are singers, Broadway actors, Wall Street traders, journalists, and aspiring authors. They are curious, searching for answers to all kinds of questions, especially this one: Can we really trust the Lord with every aspect of our lives — or with just a few select areas? In order to live in cooperation with the Holy Spirit and be fully liberated in a spiritual sense from life's burdens, we must not hold back any aspect of our lives from the Lord.

When We Worry about the Wrong Things

We have a saying in our house that it's always a good idea to major in the majors — to make the main thing the main thing. It's all too easy to get agitated over issues that are actually quite minor and hardly worth our worry. In fact, I would go so far as to suggest that the "miserable Christian" is more often than not getting sidetracked by minor issues. They're finding the negative within the positive.

Case in point: I write a daily blog and try to take a few snapshots of the culture throughout the course of the week. I comment on everything from movies to sports to critical social issues such as the sanctity of life and the definition of marriage. I've come to realize that I get much higher readership for matters related to pop culture, gossip, and topics such as whether dogs and cats go to heaven. I appreciate the interest in "juicy news" items, but I wonder if we're too easily distracted by issues that are of a temporal nature? For example, think about how upset people become over the choice of worship music in church. Entire churches have split over the matter of hymns versus praise songs. Or how about our choice of clothing on Sunday morning? Does it matter what we wear to church?!

A colleague broached this question recently, and it reminded me of my early days as a Christian at Calvary Chapel in Southern California. By the time I accepted Christ in high school, the hippie movement was near its end, as was the Jesus movement — a dynamic uprising of young Christians whose style of worship was quite unconventional. Where I lived, many of these new believers were surfers and beach people. They were hungry for the Lord, but they weren't interested in anything traditional

— especially getting all dressed up for church in neatly pressed suits and dress clothes.

The pastor was Chuck Smith, whose background intrigued me. In 1965, years before we met, Chuck was the pastor of a small church in Newport Beach. He and his wife, Kay, would drive around the streets of Newport and Laguna Beach and watch the passing parade of young people, many of whom were on drugs and, quite literally and figuratively, lost. At first, Chuck became angry, lamenting the waste of human potential he saw. But Kay's reaction was much different, and it convicted her young husband.

"You know, they are so desperately in need of Jesus," she said to him one day.

Chuck and Kay began to witness to some of the hippies stumbling by, and before long, his church was filled with them. Calvary Chapel quickly outgrew its space and decided to build a new facility.

Not everyone felt comfortable worshiping alongside long-haired men and women with BO. Some of the young people even came in their bare feet, which especially irked some of the traditionalists in the congregation. Chuck recalled the boiling point:

> I came to church on one Sunday morning and I saw a sign on the front that said, "No bare feet allowed." It was signed by the board. I was fortunate to be there early and I took the sign down and I called a board meeting and I told them, "Do you mean to say because we have this beautiful new carpet, we've got to say to one kid that he can't come in because you've got bare feet? Let's rip up the carpet and

have concrete floors." I also said, "If you have to say to them that they can't come because they have dirty clothes and we don't want you to soil our upholstered pews, then let's get benches and let's never, you know, turn a kid away from the church."[5]

Chuck proceeded to authorize the ripping up of the carpet, and the young people kept coming in droves. In fact, from Chuck's church an entire association of churches was born. Today, there are over one thousand Calvary Chapels around the world, and while I doubt many people show up in bare feet, I wonder how people might react if they did.

I've never believed a person's clothes should prevent them from worshiping with others, especially since God looks at the heart and not at our outward appearance (1 Samuel 16:7).

Facing the Future with Anticipation

I end this chapter with a declaration from the apostle Paul's letter to the Ephesians. "For we are God's handiwork," he wrote, "created in Christ Jesus to do good works, which God prepared in advance for us to do" (Ephesians 2:10). One of the best ways to face the uncertainty of the future with joy is to possess a spirit of anticipation. God has a job for you to do. He has it all planned out too. Are you looking up or looking down? The miserable Christian looks inward, while the joyful one looks out into the world. Author Nora Holm once observed that the happy person is usually healthy and fortunate. The world says they're happy because they are healthy and fortunate; but the truth is that they are healthy and fortunate because they are happy, because they rejoice in the Lord.[6]

Scripture *as the Rock*

Every word of God is flawless;
   he is a shield to those who take refuge in him.
Do not add to his words,
   or he will rebuke you and prove you a liar.

PROVERBS 30:5–6

HIS NAME WAS JOHN JOSEPH HUGHES, AND HE MAY HAVE been one of the most important men in American history, if not the entire world.

An Irish immigrant gardener eventually ordained to the Catholic priesthood, "Dagger John," as he was called due to the habit of punctuating his signature with a dagger-like cross and behaving with a similarly aggressive flair, became the first archbishop of the archdiocese of New York. He served between 1842 and 1864, a time of explosive Irish-Catholic growth in America. According to a reporter covering him during his tenure as the city's Catholic shepherd, he was "more a Roman gladiator than a devout follower of the meek founder of Christianity."[1]

A Protestant convert who emigrated from Ireland at age twenty, Hughes had his initial application for the priesthood rejected. Church leaders deemed him uneducated and ignorant, charges that couldn't have been further from the truth. In fact, he was brilliant and resourceful, traits that would come in handy throughout his long and productive ministry. Hughes's prowess was eventually noticed as he toiled in the church gardens. Elizabeth Ann Seton, a Catholic nun who would become the first native-born American citizen to be canonized by the Catholic Church, saw in him what everyone else had missed. Assigned to the diocese of Philadelphia after his ordination, Hughes made his mark as an eloquent orator speaking persuasively against religious bigotry. At the time, prejudice against newly arriving immigrants, especially the Irish, was rampant — for somewhat understandable reasons.

In 1838, at the age of forty, Bishop Hughes was transferred to New York, where he was appointed to the role of coadjutor bishop. His assignment couldn't have been more fraught with difficulty. Writing in the *City Journal*, a publication of the Manhattan Institute, a New York-based think tank, William Stern described the debauchery and cultural chaos found throughout the city, especially in those areas populated by recent immigrants hailing from Ireland:

> New York's Irish truly formed an underclass; every variety of social pathology flourished luxuriantly among them. Family life had disintegrated ...
>
> The immigrants crowded into neighborhoods like Sweeney's Shambles in the city's fourth ward and Five Points in the sixth ward (called the "bloody sixth" for its violence) ... Besides rampant alcoholism, addiction to opium and laudanum was epidemic in these neighborhoods in the 1840s and 1850s. Many Irish immigrants communicated in their own profanity-filled street slang called "flash talk": a multi-day drinking spree was "going

on a bender," "cracking a can" was robbing a house. Literate English practically disappeared from ordinary conversation.

An estimated 50,000 Irish prostitutes, known in flash talk as "nymphs of the pave," worked the city in 1850, and Five Points alone had as many as seventeen brothels. Illegitimacy reached stratospheric heights — and tens of thousands of abandoned Irish kids roamed, or prowled, the city's streets. Violent Irish gangs, with names like the Forty Thieves, the B'boys, the Roach Guards, and the Chichesters, brought havoc to their neighborhoods. The gangs fought one another and the nativists — but primarily they robbed houses and small businesses, and trafficked in stolen property. Over half the people arrested in New York in the 1840s and 1850s were Irish, so that police vans were dubbed "paddy wagons" and episodes of mob violence in the streets were called "donnybrooks," after a town in Ireland.

Death was everywhere. In 1854 one out of every 17 people in the sixth ward died. In Sweeney's Shambles the rate was one out of five in a 22-month period. The death rate among Irish families in New York in the 1850s was 21 percent, while among non-Irish it was 3 percent. Life expectancy for New York's Irish averaged under 40 years. Tuberculosis, which Bishop Hughes called the "natural death of the Irish immigrants," was the leading cause of death, along with drink and violence.[2]

This was the horrendous scene into which the new bishop waded. One can only imagine what went through his head. Where to begin? For starters, he decided to build from scratch a Catholic school system, believing that the future of the city would be found in the character and intellect of its children. "In our age the question of education," he said, "is the question of the church."[3] He wanted the schools to stand out from their secular counterparts. In addition to a strict but standard curriculum based on the classical education model, the schools emphasized morality, virtue, and, naturally, Catholic theology. Parents were obligated to participate in the care and upkeep of the schools. Hughes would eventually expand his pioneering efforts to the college level, founding Fordham University, as well as Manhattan, Manhattanville, and Mount St. Vincent colleges.

But the bishop was considered to be most effective and influential when engaging New Yorkers both from the pulpit and on the street with straightforward spiritual perspective. He regularly preached on the need for personal transformation, encouraging the faithful to assume individual responsibility for their actions and realize the benefits of living disciplined and biblically grounded lives. He made the Scriptures real and relevant. The simple principles of right and wrong were stressed, which, though obvious in hindsight, seemed to have been forgotten or, at the least, regularly ignored. By all accounts, Hughes preached a simple and positive message of faith, hope, and love. By helping New Yorkers see their lives from an eternal rather than a temporal perspective, they were motivated to immediate action. His success was stunning:

> Alcoholism and drug addiction withered away. By the 1880s an estimated 60 percent of Irish women, and almost a third of the men, totally abstained from alcohol. Many

Irish sections in the city became known for their peacefulness, order, and cleanliness — a far cry from the filth, violence, and disease of the Five Points and Sweeney's Shambles of mid-century. Gone, too, was the notorious Irish promiscuity of those years; New York's Irish became known by the latter part of the nineteenth century as a churched people, often chided by the press for their "puritanical" attitudes. Irish prostitutes virtually disappeared in the city, as did the army of Irish youths wandering the streets without adult supervision. Irish family life, formerly so frayed and chaotic, became strong and nourishing. Irish children entered the priesthood or the convent, the professions, politics, professional sports, show business, and commerce. In 1890 some 30 percent of New York City's teachers were Irish women, and the Irish literacy rate exceeded 90 percent. In 1871 reformer "Honest" John Kelly became the leader of Tammany Hall, and with the election in 1880 of shipping magnate William Grace as mayor, the Irish assumed control of city politics.[4]

The city had been transformed, not by fiat or fire and brimstone, but through the deliberate and disciplined efforts of a man whose main goal was to change a culture by reforming hearts and minds in and through the name of Jesus Christ. He didn't simply preach at them; he talked with them, like a father to a son. And the effects of this direct and gracious approach are still being felt today. Experts have suggested that had Bishop Hughes failed in his attempt to reform the Catholic Irish culture in New York, the future of American immigration and thus, America itself, would have been drastically altered.

There's reason to believe this analysis is correct, and here's why: As I've noted, blame for New York's cultural decay and rampant immorality was primarily, if not entirely, being pinned on the newly arrived Irish immigrants. In response, the idea of shutting down the borders altogether was gaining support. In fact, many saw this action as the only valid option to stem the terrible tide of bad behavior. But instead of getting rid of the troublemakers, Hughes and the faithful changed not only the behavior of these individuals but also their worldview. And in the end, they helped shape the future of America in an immensely positive manner. If advocates for closing the borders had succeeded, the more than 23 million immigrants who arrived on the nation's shores between 1881 and 1920 would never had made it here, thus depriving the United States one of its greatest treasures — the diversity of its people.

It may seem reasonable to discount this example of cultural transformation as something from another era. But to dismiss it so quickly would be a grave mistake. Those committed to redeeming the current culture can find practical application and inspiration in the work of Bishop John Hughes. Although a man of significant title, he possessed no extraordinary authority or talent. He could talk and teach with power and persuasion — but many had previously attempted to impact the culture in that manner, only to fail. What made Hughes different was that instead of trying to merely change behavior, he worked tirelessly to reach a person's heart and thus their motivational center. He was able to craft arguments and share information in a way that moved people from apathy to action. And most importantly, as he did this, he was able to effect permanent change.

It's tempting for Christians to engage the culture in the way many of us were schooled in evangelism fundamentals. When the late Bill Bright composed the four spiritual laws in 1952, Christians welcomed the tract's powerful simplicity and straightforward approach. But I wonder if it ever struck you that these four key truths don't necessarily lead to behavioral and heart change. Let's review them:

1. God loves you and offers a wonderful plan for your life. (JOHN 3:16; 10:10)

2. Man is sinful and separated from God. Therefore he cannot know and experience God's love and plan for his life. (ROMANS 3:23; 6:23)

3. Jesus Christ is God's only provision for man's sin. Through Him you can know and experience God's love and plan for your life. (JOHN 14:6; ROMANS 5:8; 1 CORINTHIANS 15:3 – 6)

4. We must individually receive Jesus Christ as Savior and Lord; then we can know and experience God's love and plan for our lives. (JOHN 1:12; 3:1 – 8; EPHESIANS 2:8 – 9; REVELATION 3:20)[5]

I don't disagree with any of these "laws," but it's possible for new believers to embrace these words, and even their essence, but not actually change their behavior. This is why we often hear about "lapsed" Christians who struggle with old and bad habits. Belief doesn't always impact behavior. If we're truly interested in engaging and transforming the culture, we must try to change the hearts and minds of the people within the culture itself.

Together They Pushed Until the Walls Fell

Ronald Reagan biographer and former speechwriter Peggy Noonan recently reflected on the reasons that her former boss succeeded at tasks his predecessors and colleagues had repeatedly failed at. Winning the Cold War and reunifying Europe were monumental achievements, and according to Noonan, they didn't come easily, quickly, or without help. Noonan wrote, "Good people picked good leaders — the Big Three of the Cold War, Margaret Thatcher, Pope John Paul II, Reagan — and together they pushed until walls fell."[6] In other words, Reagan was joined by other good people who possessed a sound character and a spirit of persistence. They simply didn't give up. Like Bishop Hughes, they didn't grow weary in their assigned tasks, and they changed a country, the culture, and a world by first changing the hearts and minds of its leaders.

The history of Christian engagement is marked by similar characteristics. It's been said that all good things come slowly, and never has this been truer than in the life and times of those who claim to be Christ-followers. I am reminded of abolitionist William Wilberforce's prolonged campaign to end slavery. In a stirring speech before the House of Commons, the British politician declared, "God Almighty has set before me two great objects, the suppression of the slave trade and the reformation of manners (morality)."

Wilberforce went on to affirm a commitment to the cause, no matter how long it would take:

> This is the first fruits of our efforts; let us persevere and our triumph will be *complete*. Never, never will we desist till we have wiped away this scandal from the Christian

name, released ourselves from the load of guilt, under which we at present labor, and extinguished every trace of this bloody traffic, of which our posterity, looking back to the history of these enlightened times, will scarce believe that it has been suffered to exist so long a disgrace and dishonor to this country.[7]

Patience Is the Companion of Wisdom

Nothing can take the place of persistence. It is, of course, important to do the right things for the right reasons — but in the doing, we must resign ourselves to the often protracted nature of the challenges that face us. Patience doesn't come easily, especially in a world that demands everything right now. According to some scholars, it was patience (*makrothymia* in the Greek) that strengthened the Roman Empire. The Romans never compromised with or yielded to their enemies, even in defeat. Instead, they stood firm, like a boulder embedded in a stream. They were not afraid to let the waters pass over them, content to take the slings and arrows as long as they were convinced they were standing on solid moral ground.

One of my favorite chapters in all of Scripture is found in the letter to the Hebrews. There is such wonderful perspective in chapter 11, this "Hall of Faith" chapter in which we're reminded of the biblical heroes and other believers who didn't experience "success" while on this earth. In speaking of many Old Testament key figures, the biblical writer states, "These all died in faith, not having received the things promised, but having seen them and greeted them from afar, and having acknowledged that they were strangers and exiles on the earth" (Hebrews 11:13 ESV). And then after we are told of the nameless individuals who were tortured, pelted with stones, and sawed in two, we read this word of ultimate hope: "These were all commended for their faith, yet none of them received what was promised, since God had planned something better for us so that only together with us would they be made perfect" (Hebrews 11:39 – 40).

Engagement Comes at a Price

Whenever we engage the culture, we will invariably rub some people the wrong way. Writing to the Galatians, Paul couldn't have been clearer: "Am I now trying to win the approval of human beings, or of God?" he asked rhetorically. "Or am I trying to please people? If I were still trying to please people, I would not be a servant of Christ" (Galatians 1:10). He's right. As believers, we may not win many battles — but we're not engaging to win. Our motive is not power. We simply — but quite profoundly — engage because we want the culture to reflect God's glory.

I know how difficult this can be. It's not instinctual. When someone takes a swing at us, it's natural to want to respond in kind. When I've stepped out and dialogued with people holding a different perspective, I've often taken it in the chops. The hard part is remaining open to consider what my critics have to say without becoming angry, defensive, and combative. At the same time, I've learned that there comes a point where it doesn't matter what I say or do in response to them. Unless I parrot their message verbatim or take their recommended course of action, they will not be satisfied. In other words, some people don't want a dialogue or conversation; they simply want to tell the rest of us what we're doing wrong. The implication is that they are not only doing things the godly, biblical, Jesus-pleasing, right way, but that they must enforce the same code of behavior in others to prove their own depth of conviction.

However, telling others what they're doing wrong without engaging in open dialogue amounts to nothing more than legalism and Pharisaic self-righteousness; it certainly isn't an expression of a winsome faith that reflects the loving heart of God. Sadly, many people insist on representing God this way — as if a shouting match, angry sound bite, or well-crafted condemnation could invite anyone to know Him. And if we're honest, we, too, may have represented God — and what we believe He wants — in this same abrasive way.

If we are going to reclaim the essence of the gospel and change public perception about what it means to be a Christian, it will take a lesson in communication. It will require a willingness to have a conversation instead of preaching to the choir. It will mean active and respectful listening. It will involve not only thinking before we speak but also praying before we think.

The Medium Is the Massage

Since becoming president of Focus on the Family, I've been privileged to participate in many interviews and appear on numerous media programs to discuss the mission of the ministry. I've spoken with people on the right, on the left, and everywhere in between. The majority of the exchanges have been pleasant, and even those writers and reporters with strong ideological inclinations have, for the most part, been fair. During one television news program, though, I was surprised at the degree of theater exhibited throughout the exchange. The host played both good cop and bad cop with the three guests — but during commercial breaks, he dropped the cantankerous persona and began discussing dinner plans with the seeming villain of the segment — a Democrat strategist.

After the interview, I chastised myself for expecting more — after all, the show's goal is to attract more viewers, thus allowing stations that broadcast it to charge their advertisers higher fees. The way to do this is to be outrageous and bombastic, to make the listeners' blood pressure go up for one reason or another. I shouldn't expect the show's tone to be thoughtful, compassionate, challenging, and edifying, right?

Examining my expectations brings to mind the truth that much of what we hear is shaped by how and where we hear it. Marshall McLuhan's famous pronouncement that "the medium is the message" continues to take on new dimensions in our world of Facebook, Twitter, e-books, and texting.[8] Having coined the phrase "the global village" and envisioning the Internet thirty years before it existed, McLuhan believed the vehicle for any message — its medium — embeds itself in the content delivery of the message itself.

For example, consider the difference between receiving a party invitation engraved on heavy linen paper in the mail and receiving the same invitation in an e-mail. They both refer to the same event, using identical words, but most people perceive the engraved invitation as being more formal, elegant, and extravagant. This perception then affects their expectation of the event itself, even if it is only a neighborhood cookout. Or consider the difference between an editorial in *The Washington Post* and one in the *Walla Walla Union-Bulletin* (no offense).

McLuhan went on to write a book that intended to feature his most famous phrase as its title. However, due to a printing error, the book became *The Medium Is the Massage*, which amused him so much in its reinterpretation that he kept it as the final title. This accidental word change may describe our current cultural communications even better than McLuhan's original phrasing. Every message gets massaged in its presentation; every public communication seems to have a spin. Whether it's a network news report, magazine advertisement, celebrity sound bite, or politico's blog entry, the way information is conveyed influences us and our perception of the communicator's intentions.

In a world of sound bites, a memorable phrase, catchy slogan, or infectious jingle can be worth millions of dollars. If I encourage you to "just do it," it's tough not to think of Nike. With a question like "Where's the beef?" the old Wendy's commercial comes to mind. Historical events are often captured the same way. Some of you will know exactly what I mean when I mention such phrases as "a date that will live in infamy," "I am not a crook!" or "If it doesn't fit, you must acquit." Or consider presidential campaign slogans such as "Read my lips — no new taxes!" or "Yes, we can!"

The Bible is clear on how Christians are to speak to others. The book of Proverbs is filled with wisdom, insight, and instruction on how we are to use our words in God-honoring ways. We're told that God hates lying and deceit (6:17 – 19; 12:22), that flattery harms those who give as well as receive it (26:28; 29:5), that gossip similarly poisons the speaker and listener (11:13; 17:9), and that cursing reveals the sinfulness in us more than the recipient of our foul words (20:20; 30:10). Perhaps Proverbs 15:4 (NIV, 1984 edition) sums it up best: "The tongue that brings healing is a tree of life, but a deceitful tongue crushes the spirit."

The New Testament book of James emphasizes the power of the tongue to both destroy like a wildfire or guide like the rudder of a boat. James describes the tongue as a "restless evil, full of deadly poison," which no one can completely tame (3:8). His conclusion focuses on the way our tongues reveal who we are and what's inside us.

> With the tongue we praise our Lord and Father, and with it we curse human beings, who have been made in God's likeness. Out of the same mouth come praise and cursing. My brothers and sisters, this should not be. Can both fresh water and salt water flow from the same spring?
>
> JAMES 3:9–11

Perhaps we could ask the question this way: Are we accurately reflecting God's heart and the love of Christ when we judge others and pronounce condemnation? Do other people truly glimpse the Lord we love and serve when we attack politicians and make jokes about their beliefs?

Again, God's Word is clear about how we are to live out our faith, including how we are to watch what we say:

> And the Lord's servant must not be quarrelsome but must be kind to everyone, able to teach, not resentful. Opponents must be gently instructed, in the hope that God

will grant them repentance leading them to a knowledge of the truth, and that they will come to their senses and escape from the trap of the devil, who has taken them captive to do his will.

2 TIMOTHY 2:24–26

It's striking that this passage does not say we should loudly dismiss or joyfully condemn those who oppose us. We are to gently instruct, with the goal that God (not us!) will allow them a knowledge of the truth — again, *His truth*, not our interpretation of truth that day. Paul's rhetorical question in his letter to the Christians in Rome summarizes it well: "Or do you show contempt for the riches of [God's] *kindness*, forbearance and patience, not realizing that God's *kindness* is intended to lead you to repentance?" (Romans 2:4, emphasis mine). No wonder then in his letter to the church at Ephesus, Paul exhorts, "Do not let any unwholesome talk come out of your mouths, but only what is helpful for building others up according to their needs, that it may benefit those who listen" (Ephesians 4:29).

Sadly, we often fall into the trap of wanting to be right rather than wanting to love well. Please understand that loving well, being kind, and gently instructing doesn't mean being soft, turning a blind eye, or giving in whenever someone opposes the example and teachings of Christ. It doesn't mean we aren't willing to express our views or be clear on what Scripture says about various issues. However, it does mean we must examine the motives of our hearts. If we're merely determined to reinforce our own beliefs or please our peers at church or judge someone else so we can feel better about ourselves, then we're in real trouble.

The Sound Bite of Silence

I'm convinced that the best way to ground our speech in love is to care more about people than about getting their admission that we're right. Yes, we are to uphold the beliefs of the orthodox Christian faith (more about this in the next chapter), but not at the expense of compromising our reflection of God's character and Christ's love. My basis for this belief comes from Jesus and His example in addressing the pious religious leaders of His day, the Pharisees and Sadducees, who often tried to trap Him by citing the laws of Scripture. Their desperate need to be right and respected blinded them to the heart of God.

Jesus consistently sidestepped and turned their traps on them by drilling down to the intention and essence of the law. When the Pharisees baited Him with questions such as "Don't you know you and your disciples should be washing your hands before handling bread?" Jesus responded with a question that put them on the hook: "Don't you know you shouldn't confuse your legalistic traditions with God's commandments?" (see Matthew 15:1 – 9).

On another occasion, the legalistic religious leaders saw Jesus and His disciples picking grain and eating it on the Sabbath day and delighted in giving them a Jewish speeding ticket (see Matthew 12:1 – 2). Jesus responded by reminding them about exceptions — David and his hungry soldiers entering God's house and eating consecrated bread; the temple priests who desecrated the Sabbath laws and yet were innocent (Matthew 12:3 – 8). Jesus knew they weren't concerned about keeping God's laws out of respect, humility, and honor, but they were fixated on discrediting Jesus and elevating themselves.

The Pharisees consistently wanted to make godliness about what one does. Jesus consistently made it clear that godliness is about why one does what one does. People focus on externals; God focuses on our hearts.

So if we are not to jump to conclusions and shout down those who oppose us, then what *are* we supposed to do? As Jesus did, so we must consistently pause to listen to our Father's voice. In fact, after telling His disciples a parable, Jesus urges them, "Consider carefully how you listen" (Luke 8:18). God speaks a similar message about how we should consider Jesus: "This is my Son, whom I love. Listen to him!" (Mark 9:7).

At the risk of trivializing this critical point, I'm reminded of the simple yet life-saving adage posted at old railroad crossings: Stop, Look, and Listen. I wonder if it would serve us well if we were to pause when we come to a place of potential conflict, look to our heavenly Father for guidance, and then listen to Him, as well as to those across the tracks from us. Too often we lower the crossing gates and sound the alarms, determined to segregate ourselves from the viewpoints of others instead of realizing that neither of us has to be thrown in front of the train.

Our communication about anything related to our faith — and therefore, about everything — must begin with the sound bite of silence. We must consistently be still before God and acknowledge our awe at who He is, what He has done for us through Jesus Christ, and what He continues to do through His Spirit. In her book *The Art of Spiritual Listening*, Alice Fryling reminds us that recognizing the voice of Jesus is a learned art. It requires prayer, discernment, Bible study, input from others, and silence. "Part of our spiritual journey" writes Fryling, "is learning to listen to God, to pay attention to the gentle whispers of God's Holy Spirit."[9]

My fear is that in our dogged pursuit of orthodoxy — defining it, explaining it, defending it — we have lost the art of listening to God so that we may speak His loving truth. How often do we stop and ask God what He would like us to communicate to those who hold opposing views? How often do we presume to know what God wants us to say to people from another political party, from a different branch of the Christian faith, from a different religion altogether? How many of us spend more time praying for our enemies than arguing with them?

A Final Word about the Millennial Generation

I've never lamented that the future of the Christian church rests in the hands of those from Generation X, Y, or now Z. I've always believed there are great leaders in every age and stage of life — you just need to know where to look.

Esther Fleece, Focus on the Family's director of Millennial relations, is a leader who has helped Focus partner with many like-minded ministries dedicated to reaching the next generation. Since joining our team, Esther has done a masterful job engaging those in their twenties and thirties. She has discovered that while many of them share our values, many do not. Thom Rainer, the president of Lifeway Christian Resources, and his Millennial son, Jess, wrote a book about the Millennial Generation. Here's what they found out:

- Few Millennials consider religion/spiritual issues to be important. The majority are not hostile toward Christianity, but apathetic.

- While two-thirds claim to adhere to some form of Christianity, only about 15 percent would fit any sort of biblical definition of "Christian."

- The great majority of Millennials are weary of polarization in families, politics, and religion, and they highly value civility, respect, and a willingness to listen.

- Millennials have a strong desire to serve, and Christian Millennials gravitate to churches that have an outward focus.

- Most Millennials have a syncretistic belief system — they cobble together their spiritual understanding and values from an array of sources.

- Most have a generally positive view of Jesus as they understand Him, but their image of Jesus is often uninformed by Scripture.

- Millennials tend to follow and amplify the pattern of their parents in matters of faith. Those who grew up in a nominally Christian home often abandon the faith altogether, while those who had a strong Christian upbringing tend to become even more fervent.

- Diluted doctrine and anemic biblical teaching and preaching are huge turnoffs for most Millennial Christians.

- Millennial Christians seek transparency, humility, and integrity in leaders.[10]

I'm well aware of the cultural challenges facing us, and yet I read these findings with a renewed sense of purpose. What tremendous opportunity to reach this next generation if we are

willing to engage them! The Lord holds and controls everything, including all time and space. We don't have to be anxious
about the future. God does not want us to become pleasant,
passive, and accepting of everything as we interact with and
speak into the world around us. Nor does He want us to be
obnoxious, antagonistic, and judgmental. God only asks us to
speak His truth from hearts grounded in love. "Let your conversation be always full of grace, seasoned with salt, so that you
may know how to answer everyone" (Colossians 4:6). Particularly in the public forum, let us speak with an irresistible aroma
that whets the spiritual appetite of all who hear us.

10

The Kindness of God
Leads to Repentance

For our struggle is not against flesh and blood,
but against the rulers, against the authorities,
against the powers of this dark world and against
the spiritual forces of evil in the heavenly realms.

EPHESIANS 6:12

As I already mentioned, my upbringing did nothing to prepare me for my role as the leader of the largest family-based Christian ministry in the world, yet it did *everything*. My life continues to unfold as God's beautiful mosaic, a work of art that only He could design, working with the broken pieces of my childhood, my family of origin, and my longing for a place called home.

As one of five kids, I learned at an early age that our house wasn't a safe place. My parents were alcoholics — in fact, they met at AA. Unfortunately, their sobriety was intermittent and led to bitter arguments and eventually to their divorce when I was five. Many years passed before I saw my father again. My mother remarried a man I nicknamed "Hank the Tank," an ex-Navy man who loved blind obedience, cleanliness, ordered precision, and strict punishments.

When my mother died of cancer a couple years after marrying Hank, my world dissolved like a sidewalk chalk drawing after a rain shower. Hank had always considered the five of us excess baggage, so it was no surprise after Mom's death that he left us to fend for ourselves. With a father who ran out on us and a stepfather who didn't want us, the count was 0 and 2. The foster family we moved in with next, the Reils, quickly made it clear that I had struck out. While I eventually reunited with my dad, he continued to battle alcoholism and depression, a battle he would lose by the time I was twelve years old.

I know what it means both to be an orphan and to experience the love of God through the kindness, compassion, and caring of other people. When I look back on my life, I see my heavenly Father's loving-kindness expressed through many people's actions. I don't remember much of what they said, but I'll never forget the families of friends who put out an extra plate at their table and invited me to stay for dinner and the teachers who took time to help me focus on schoolwork amid the many distractions I faced at home. My high school football coach, Paul Moro, demonstrated what it meant to follow Jesus on and off the field. He taught me that serving God and others is what this life is all about. He took great delight in serving teenagers and helping them along the way, and he is still helping and serving kids today. In fact, Paul was named national football coach of the year by the National High School Athletic Coaches Association in 2011. Well deserved!

Supermodels of Faith

As followers of Christ, we are called to be supermodels — not glamorous stars walking the runways of fashion but flesh-and-blood men and women walking the streets of daily despair with the good news of God's love. Our lifestyles, decisions, and actions must exemplify and align with our thoughts, words, and beliefs. To live out this authentic faith, we must integrate our minds, our hearts, and our actions.

As I understand Scripture and theology, our Christian faith is supported by three pillars: an understanding of God's character and truth, largely drawn from His Word; an ongoing relationship with Him through the presence and guidance of His Holy Spirit; and a lifestyle of actions, behavior, and service based on the life of Jesus. Another way to express this triad is that the Christian faith is in our heads (knowledge and understanding of truth), our hearts (communication and direction from the Holy Spirit), and our actions (Christlike behavior and servant leadership). Our spiritual growth is tied directly to these three — our beliefs about, our awareness of, and our obedience to God.

As a visual learner, one picture that helps me appreciate the way these three pieces interact is a seesaw. On one end is our head knowledge — thoughts, beliefs, and convictions about God. On the other end is the way in which we live out this understanding in daily life. The fulcrum in the middle is the Holy Spirit, to whom we must be attuned if we are to remain in balance. If our Christian walk doesn't match our talk, we will crash on one end. If we only perform good deeds but fail to be in relationship with the Source of all that is good, we will collapse on the other side.

Jesus made it clear that a life of legalism — essentially the way the Pharisees and religious leaders of that day related to God — did not honor the Father. They believed that as long as they kept the Levitical law and followed the traditional Jewish rituals, they were righteous. Jesus maintained that God looks at our hearts and not on the public persona we artfully contrive to fool those around us and even ourselves. When confronting the Pharisees, Jesus didn't mince words: "Woe to you, teachers of the law and Pharisees, you hypocrites! You are like white-washed tombs, which look beautiful on the outside but on the inside are full of the bones of the dead and everything unclean" (Matthew 23:27).

During a recent Focus on the Family board of directors meeting, we discussed this very topic. One of the participants mentioned the need to balance truth and grace. Dr. Al Mohler, president of Southern Seminary in Louisville, Kentucky, dis-agreed with the statement, though not the sentiment. He pointed out that since truth and grace are inseparable, it's not a matter of balance. In essence, truth is grace, and grace is truth. They are one and the same. His statement struck me as pro-foundly accurate.

James warns us, along with the apostle Paul, that following Jesus isn't just a matter of what we say we believe. No, what we claim to believe must be backed up by lives that align with these beliefs. Apparently, some of the new Christians in the early churches were talking a good game but not living it. James explains:

> Do not merely listen to the word, and so deceive your-
> selves. Do what it says. Anyone who listens to the word
> but does not do what it says is like someone who looks at
> his face in a mirror and, after looking at himself, goes away
> and immediately forgets what he looks like. But whoever
> looks intently into the perfect law that gives freedom, and

> continues in it — not forgetting what they have heard, but
> doing it — they will be blessed in what they do.
>
> JAMES 1:22 – 25

I fear that our contemporary Christian faith has gotten out of balance. We seem to spend a lot of time, especially in the public forum, talking about what it means to be a real Christian. At its worst, we come across as narrow (if not closed-minded), self-righteous, and judgmental. Best-case scenario, we speak truth and explain the message of the gospel. However, in our contemporary fifteen-second sound bite culture, our actions will always speak louder than words. Whether or not we think people are paying attention, we can be assured that everyone around us is acutely aware of how we live, especially if we call ourselves followers of Jesus.

While we are called to be a "peculiar people" who are set apart from the world and its standards (Titus 2:14; 1 Peter 2:9), too often Christians build a hedge around their lives and feel compelled to defend themselves like a moat around a castle. When we condemn political candidates for something they said or call for a boycott of businesses because of a cause they support, are we truly reflecting the heart of God? Or could there be clearer, stronger ways to communicate God's character and His standards (holy and life-giving)?

Spiritually Mugged

I have a good friend about the same age who had kids at a much younger age than I did. As a result, my buddy Phil seems much older, since his four kids are all young adults. In fact, he hit a major milestone recently when his oldest son married, the first of his children to "leave and cleave." I've had fun hearing Phil share about the ups (heart-to-heart talks) and downs (the cost!) of helping launch his son's new life as a married man.

One story continues to stand out in my mind. Phil's son now works and lives in Tennessee (he grew up in Colorado). The bride and her family live in Tennessee, while Phil and the rest of the groom's family live in Colorado. So for his son's bachelor party, Phil traveled to Nashville with his other son and several of the groom's high school friends and college buddies. They stayed at a posh downtown hotel, and they made plans to attend a Nashville Predators – Colorado Avalanche hockey game on that Saturday night.

After checking in on Friday night, Phil and the guys strolled down Broadway Street a few blocks from their hotel to a local restaurant and bar that featured live country and bluegrass music. Being in Music City, they figured they should experience country music firsthand, and this place came highly recommended from multiple sources. On the way they passed numerous other bars and restaurants, along with a strip club, a pawn shop, and a couple tattoo parlors.

As they reached the block where the restaurant was located, they noticed a handful of people across the street holding up signs and shouting out. As Phil and the bachelor party got closer, they saw the signs: "Repent or Burn"; "The Wages of Sin Is Death — And You're Working Overtime"; "Hell Is Real." The small group of evangelists shouted out similar messages accompanied by the quoting of assorted Bible verses.

Phil and his family are strong Christians, but he knew that some of his son's friends were not. As they got closer to their destination, the ten guys in the bachelor party became the focus of the street preachers. While the young men tried to ignore the angry hollering, Phil smiled and waved, bold to acknowledge his faith and hoping to salvage the non-Christians' impressions. In fact, Phil decided to go over and talk with the three men and two women who were deeply passionate about their faith.

After speaking with them for ten minutes, Phil soon realized they weren't willing to believe he was a Christian. One of them even said, "Sir, if you were a *true* Christian, you would not be entering an establishment dedicated to alcohol, debauchery, and immorality." These guys obviously didn't know my friend Phil, because to him these were fighting words. He responded, "If *you* were true Christians, you'd be serving dinner down at the rescue mission instead of making assumptions and heckling tourists. It's easy to judge someone by their appearance, but it takes holy humility to serve those in need." He then turned and walked away, as someone in the group called out after him, "We'll pray for your salvation!"

Phil shared this incident with me the following week and acknowledged that he didn't handle the situation well. "It just makes me so angry, Jim," he said. "Did those folks really think a nonbeliever would walk up to them and say, 'Oh, I didn't realize I was going to hell until I saw your sign! Please tell me what I need to do to be saved just like you!' One of the guys in our group — a nonbeliever — told me that he felt spiritually mugged and laughed about it. He felt beat-up, not invited to hear good news."

My friend continued. "Don't get me wrong — I'm not against street evangelism or setting up an outpost in enemy territory. I just wonder if those guys I encountered were there for the benefit of others or for themselves." I agreed with Phil's assessment and wondered how I would've handled the situation. Because of my high visibility as the leader of Focus, I try to be thoughtful about the places where I'm seen in public. Yet I also know that Jesus wasn't afraid to risk his reputation in order to love everyone — sinners, prostitutes, lepers, and tax collectors included.

At a deeper level, I found Phil's comment compelling. Aren't we prone to do things in the name of Jesus so we can feel better about ourselves and prove we're "really Christians" instead of acting humbly and compassionately for the true benefit of those around us? It's not my place to judge the few evangelists on that street in Nashville. I wasn't there, and I know that God can and does use street preaching to draw people to Him. However, when someone feels spiritually mugged as a result of simply walking by them, it speaks volumes.

Hard to Find

When I was in college, I was intrigued by how our professors handled issues intersecting with personal belief and faith in God — in other words, issues pertaining to everything! In one of my English classes, we read a few short stories written by Flannery O'Connor, a Southern woman who lived out her Christian faith as a Catholic. Miss O'Connor fascinated me, in part because of her wry sense of humor and also because of the way she incorporated her faith into her writings. The story I remember best is "A Good Man Is Hard to Find" — the story of a typical Southern family, which includes a husband and wife, two kids (a son and a daughter), a new baby, and a grandmother (the father's mother who lived with them).[1]

It's summertime, and they are on the way to Florida for vacation, all six of them crammed in a station wagon, along with the grandmother's pet Siamese cat, Pitty-Sing. Prior to their leaving, two important pieces of information are revealed. The first is that the grandmother is a "good Christian woman," a lifelong believer known for her deep and abiding faith in Jesus. Second, a crew of escaped convicts is on the loose, and among them is a notorious killer nicknamed "The Misfit."

If you've ever taken a road trip as a child or parent, you can imagine the emotional atmosphere inside this family's car. The father is on a mission to drive as long as they can without stopping. The mother has to take on the role of peacemaker, trying to keep the kids settled, the baby pacified, her mother-in-law happy, and the cat under control. The kids bicker and comment on the sights and signs they pass along the way. The baby cries and frets. The grandmother chatters away, often making condescending and even racist remarks about people they see. Not exactly a trip to Disney World!

The grandmother remembers a big, beautiful plantation house she had visited when she was much younger and becomes fixated on taking a side trip to find it again. The father reluctantly agrees when it becomes clear that his mother will give them no peace until he sets out to find it. Long story short (since it is a short story), they get lost along the back roads of a remote rural area, their car breaks down, and the escaped convicts show up. Although she doesn't tell anyone, the grandmother realized along the way that the place they're seeking is in another state altogether!

Although there is no overt violence or graphic details, through the power of what O'Connor infers and we as readers imagine, it's clear that The Misfit and his band of convicts are killing this poor family one by one. Even as she watches her family members walk away at gunpoint, even as she hears the gunshots, the grandmother continues to chatter about how she knows The Misfit is a good man who is incapable of committing the terrible crimes of which he's been charged. She goes on and on about how he must be a Christian like she is, implying that since they share a common faith, he will let her live.

Finally, Granny is the last family member alive, and she doesn't seem fazed in the least by the deaths of her family members. It's clear that the only person she's thinking about is herself. As she keeps yammering on about how The Misfit must be a Christian, he stops her and makes it clear where he stands. He says that he has read the Bible and appreciates what Jesus is about and who He claims to be. However, since The Misfit wasn't there at the time of Jesus, he can't know for sure whether Jesus really is who He said He was. In The Misfit's worldview, the only way to know God is through concrete, firsthand, eyewitness evidence.

As the grandmother keeps on talking, she reaches out toward the murderous criminal, and he shoots her. One of the other convicts comments to The Misfit that he's glad he finally shot the old woman and made her shut up. The Misfit comments that "she would've been a good woman if there'd been someone there to shoot her every day." End of story.

After reading it the first time, I was stunned. A mixture of emotions churned inside me — horror and anger at the callous evil of The Misfit and his crew; frustration and sadness over this poor family; annoyance, amusement, and satisfaction that the grandmother got what was coming to her. The first two sets of feelings made sense to me, but the last cluster of emotions did not. Was I really just as glad as the convict that the old woman finally shut up? Did I really find satisfaction in seeing the tables turned so dramatically?

The brilliance of "A Good Man Is Hard to Find" lies in the way that O'Connor subtly unveils her themes:

- that the self-proclaimed "good Christian people" who talk about Jesus more than they act like Him might not know Him at all

- that nonbelievers, even escaped convicts who murder innocent families, often live out their beliefs with more integrity and consistency than Christians do

- that we readers are no better than the hypocritical grandmother if we end up judging her and feeling validated when her flimsy faith can't save her

- that those of us who call ourselves Christians can develop a true faith, with our actions in clear alignment with what we say we believe, in the midst of the life-and-death tests we encounter along life's road

Practice Makes Perfect

I often see this last theme emerge in the lives of Christ-followers in other countries. Often their cultures, governments, and even families are hostile to the Bible and the Christian faith. Each time members of a home church in China convene, they risk arrest and possible imprisonment. In other closed nations,

Christians risk their lives to smuggle in Bibles and share their faith with fellow citizens. Even in the United Kingdom and Europe, where there is no overt persecution of Christians, the believers I encounter are serious about their faith because they live in a post-Christian culture where traditions of the faith, including prayer and church, are considered to be old-fashioned, superstitious, and uneducated. Being a Christian will not meet with cultural validation or social acceptance; they know that following Christ is an uphill battle.

Many pastors and Christian leaders in the United States fear that our country is headed in a post-Christian direction based on our culture's declining morals, lack of biblical knowledge, and self-absorption. While I share their concern, I sometimes wonder if the upside could be worth it. People wouldn't go to church for shallow reasons — just to network or meet other nice singles, or because their families have always gone. People wouldn't read their Bibles and pray and serve in their communities just to feel good about themselves alongside their peers. Like the grandmother in "A Good Man Is Hard to Find," we may be surprised at how real our faith becomes when we're forced to respond at gunpoint.

I'm not trying to be harsh or to disrespect the millions of Christians in our country and around the world who live out their faith each and every day; I'm simply drawing us back to the basic tenet of ortho*praxy*: following Christ and living by faith takes *practice*, the practical "doing" of the Word. Loving God and obeying His Word are nothing if not practical. The Bible clearly emphasizes how God cares about the details of daily life for His children — in fact, for all of His creation, including the sparrows of the air and the lilies of the field.

So we shouldn't be surprised that Jesus focused His ministry in practical, physical ways. He turned water into wine at a wedding celebration in Cana. He blessed a couple of fish and a handful of bread and turned it into a buffet for five thousand people. He healed lepers with His touch. He spit in the mud and made a healing paste for the blind. He washed the feet of His disciples. He made them breakfast on the beach. He established a ritual of remembrance and celebration through the bread and wine of the Last Supper.

In example after example, we see that God is a God of incarnation, of word made flesh. The fact that He would send His one and only Son to be born into our world as a baby — a human baby who cried, nursed, napped, and soiled His diapers — is the greatest living proof we could desire. No wonder then that Jesus repeatedly urged His followers to put their faith into practice by serving both the physical and the spiritual needs of others. On the heels of telling parables about the ten virgins and the bags of gold, Jesus explains that He will return one day to "separate the people one from another as a shepherd separates the sheep from the goats" (Matthew 25:32). Even more interesting is the criteria He will use:

> "Then the King will say to those on his right, 'Come, you who are blessed by my Father; take your inheritance, the kingdom prepared for you since the creation of the world. For I was hungry and you gave me something to eat, I was thirsty and you gave me something to drink, I was a stranger and you invited me in, I needed clothes and you clothed me, I was sick and you looked after me, I was in prison and you came to visit me.'
>
> "Then the righteous will answer him, 'Lord, when did

we see you hungry and feed you, or thirsty and give you
something to drink? When did we see you a stranger and
invite you in, or needing clothes and clothe you? When
did we see you sick or in prison and go to visit you?'

"The King will reply, 'Truly I tell you, whatever you
did for one of the least of these brothers and sisters of
mine, you did for me.'"

MATTHEW 25:34–40

Jesus' explanation about what He desires to find in those
who claim to know Him is nothing new for His audience.
Throughout Israel's history, God made it abundantly clear how
those in need were to be treated. From the time the children
of Israel wandered in the desert following the exodus from
Egypt until the time of Jesus' birth, the Scriptures consistently instructed the Jewish people to be kind, generous, and
compassionate — just like their God. Consider just a few of the
several-dozen references in the Old Testament:

Do not take advantage of the widow or the fatherless.

(EXODUS 22:22)

[God] defends the cause of the fatherless and the widow,
and loves the foreigner residing among you, giving them
food and clothing. (DEUTERONOMY 10:18)

A father to the fatherless, a defender of widows,
    is God in his holy dwelling. (PSALM 68:5)

Whoever oppresses the poor shows contempt for their
    Maker,
    but whoever is kind to the needy honors God.

(PROVERBS 14:31)

> If you spend yourselves in behalf of the hungry
>   and satisfy the needs of the oppressed,
> then your light will rise in the darkness,
>   and your night will become like the noonday.
>
> (ISAIAH 58:10)

Following Jesus' ascension, the early church demonstrated a clear grasp of the significance of taking care of those in need. Perhaps no one in the New Testament expresses the marching orders for Christians today as beautifully as James. Earlier we reflected on his clear admonition not to merely listen to the word but to do what it says (James 1:22). He goes on to make his point even more concrete:

> Those who consider themselves religious and yet do not keep a tight rein on their tongues deceive themselves, and their religion is worthless. Religion that God our Father accepts as pure and faultless is this: to look after orphans and widows in their distress and to keep oneself from being polluted by the world.
>
> JAMES 1:26–27

The early church grew as a living organism of diverse individuals serving those around them with the love of Jesus, not as a nationalistic campaign intent on political upheaval. Amid the partisan politics, social activism, and patriotic rhetoric that surrounds us today, I know of many churches that maintain their focus on Christ by meeting the needs of widows, orphans, and those in need. A friend of mine who pastors a large church in Colorado shared that when his board of elders reaches a stalemate about an issue or can't decide how to prioritize resources, they have agreed to always return to helping widows and orphans. My pastor friend explained that focusing on the real people in need in their own community makes the rhetoric of debate dissolve and brings them back to a clear view of what Jesus would do.

Occasionally, donors who partner with us will ask me what else they can do besides write a check. No matter their age, gender, profession, or income level, when they ask for suggestions, I tell them to stretch themselves, to get their hands dirty building a church in rural Kentucky or digging a well in Rwanda. I tell them to serve food at their local rescue mission or to organize a canned food drive for their area food pantry. I tell them to befriend an older person in a nursing home, to write a letter to a soldier serving overseas, to buy and donate a dozen baseball gloves to a foster home or orphanage. I encourage them to do what Jesus did and ask them to challenge me to do the same.

11

We're Not Entitled to Run the World

Be completely humble and gentle; be patient, bearing with one another in love.

EPHESIANS 4:2

WHEN PRESIDENT BARACK OBAMA INVITED ME TO ATTEND his conference on fatherhood at the White House in June 2009, many of my friends and colleagues questioned whether it was a good idea for me to participate. Some of them questioned the sincerity of the president's motives and whether, given my role, I was going to be exploited for political purposes. I received their counsel but ultimately decided to go. I'm glad I did.

During the official presentation, the president reaffirmed the importance of fathering and the reality of the damage that is done when dads are absent from the home. I found myself relating to Obama. We're the same age, and we both grew up without fathers. He talked about the hole in his heart, and I knew exactly what he meant. I told him that we should do whatever we can do to help kids fill that void. I also applauded him for raising awareness of the issue. The rising rate of fatherlessness today marks a tragedy of epic proportions.

Despite my positive experience, not everyone saw merit

in the visit. We received e-mails, letters, and phone calls from friends who disagreed with associating the Focus name with anything related to the Obama administration. I understand this perspective, and I'm sympathetic to the rationale they offer to support it. President Obama and I disagree on nearly every major issue — from the sanctity of life to the definition of marriage to health care reform to his philosophy of taxation. But he *is* the president of the United States, and the position alone should command our respect.

There's also the human side to the equation. How should I as a Christian react to an invitation to discuss matters that are deeply meaningful to the Lord? It seemed clear that if I'm being asked to offer input on policies that can help more children, I should do so. I believe we're commanded to respond kindly and respectfully to people with whom we disagree (Isaiah 1:18; Matthew 7:12). It's not about strategy; it's about sharing God's truth. When a Christian is invited to speak into the creation of public policy, he or she should gladly accept the opportunity.

More recently, I was invited to Washington to meet with one of the president's senior advisers. Admittedly, the administration was in a full campaign mode and wanted to know how they were doing within the evangelical community. I was given an open invitation to share from my heart, and I took it. My sense was that my words received a fair hearing. We talked about many of the policies that President Obama continues to embrace. It was a frank discussion, but cordial as well.

How effective and impactful that meeting was remains to be seen. But the only reason I was invited was the relationship that has developed with members of the Obama administration. It's tedious to butt up against opposing points of view and be made to feel like the odd man out. But I've come to the conclusion that it's not my responsibility to win anything or even convince them that they're wrong. My calling is to engage people, to express a biblical perspective on an issue, to show others the love of Jesus, and to trust the outcome to Him.

Jesus Trusted God with the Outcome

The circumstances and details surrounding Jesus' ascension fascinate me. When we consider the events of the forty days between Jesus' resurrection and His return to heaven, we discern a recurring theme. Even though Jesus had told His disciples He would rise from the dead on the third day, every one of them was shocked when He did. Even though Jesus continually told them that His kingdom was not of this world, His disciples clearly viewed Him as a revolutionary who was destined to overthrow the culture's rulers. This is why Jesus' followers asked him, "Lord, are you at this time going to restore the kingdom to Israel?" (Acts 1:6). Even after three intensive years by His side, they still didn't get it! Immediately after Jesus ascended into heaven, two angels suddenly appeared beside the eleven. "Why do you stand here looking into the sky?" they asked (1:11). Despite all the signs and wonders, it would appear that the apostles were still incredulous at and confused by the magnitude of it all. I'm sure we all would have been!

When I study and analyze Jesus' behavior, I'm struck by the fact that He didn't seem to become overly frustrated by His disciples' ineptitude. Even more telling is the fact that despite their state, He trusted them enough to leave them. This is highly significant. He very well could have said, "OK, you're still not getting it. You're still incapable of running things for me here on earth. I'll delay my departure, and we'll have another go at it." But He didn't. He entrusted the care of these men and His ministry to the empowerment given them by the Holy Spirit.

So if Jesus is willing to let go of the reins of control on this world, why aren't we willing to do the same? How often have we fretted over the outcome of a particular situation — an election, an illness, a situation at work? Many of us are type A personalities who want to maintain control over every situation of life. Especially when it comes to politics, a strange thing happens. We can easily become obsessed with power, being in charge, and getting our way. I know some of you will argue, "I'm not trying to push *my* way but *the Lord's* way." While there may be some truth to that statement, we still need to closely examine how we engage, remembering that the ends never justify the means.

This Is What Happens When We Make Idols of Good Things

I enjoy the rhythm and routine of work. My satisfaction may be magnified because of the ministerial aspect of my calling, but when I honestly analyze my work behavior, I admit I may enjoy it too much. Let me explain.

Sándor Ferenczi, a Hungarian psychoanalyst and disciple of Sigmund Freud, was a keen student of human behavior. In 1919, he coined the term "Sunday neurosis" to explain why so many people become depressed or anxious on weekends.[1] Having filled their week with assignments and responsibilities, they experienced the Sabbath as a marked change of pace. For the first time in six days, his patients were forced to slow down and rest. This became the cause of great consternation for these individuals. Why? Ferenczi discovered that his patients found so much significance in their work that without it, they were less of a person and at a loss to know what to do away from the office. They had made an idol of a very good thing, namely, work.

This malady may sound highly peculiar. After all, we're led to believe that almost everyone is "working for the weekend" and relieved when it finally arrives. The reality, though, is different. With the explosion of technology, which allows us to work not only anywhere but also anytime, more people now view work as a natural part of life. Constant access to e-mail via smartphones has blurred the lines of when work stops and family/leisure begins. As a result, we begin to attach to our jobs not only our significance but also our sorrows and joys. So if the promotion doesn't come or, worse yet, the pink slip arrives, we lose our bearings, and our psyches take a major hit.

But what if you've invested your life in full-time Christian ministry? Surely this can't apply to you. And yet it does — perhaps even to a greater degree. When a pastor is removed from his pulpit, he may view the rejection not just as a difference of opinion but also as a judgment on his spiritual commitment and call. At Focus on the Family, a nonprofit ministry completely dependent on the sacrificial giving of our constituents, we've had to cut our team by several hundred employees these last few years. Although this is also happening in many other organizations forced to deal with the reality of a limping economy, behind every number is a name. I feel the loss and pain of each person. But as I have counseled and comforted many in this tight job market, you can love your work and feel good about your contribution, but if your position defines you, the problem is not with your position but with you.

I know I'm not immune to making an idol of work. I suspect I'm like a lot of other people who feel called to their particular assignment outside of the home. Although I'm convinced that I'm right where the Lord wants me, I still struggle with balancing my responsibilities as president of Focus and host of its daily radio broadcast with my time not only with Jean and the boys but, ironically, also with the Lord. There always seems to be one more thing to do — attend another meeting, host a dinner, record a broadcast, participate in a convention, give a speech, read and respond to e-mail, write a letter or book or blog post. The calendar fills up quickly, almost always with significant assignments that will hopefully make a difference in the lives of other people. How can I protect myself from making idols of very good things — even things like ministry to families?

For starters, for the last few years, I've been listening to the Bible on my iPad. I like to begin my day this way, and I will listen as I run, walk, or sit on an airplane. By listening to God's Word first thing in the morning, my perspective is rightly ordered for the remaining hours of the day. It gives me perspective. To the best of my ability, I can try to put God first by disciplining myself to think of His instruction before considering any of the day's assignments. I like the late Dr. Adrian Rogers's take on this challenge of prioritization. "If I put things between me and Christ, it is idolatry," he once stated. "If I put Christ between me and things, it is victory!"[2]

I think we more easily lay down our idols when we stop

thinking it's up to us to run the world — or there is nobody as capable as we are to try to run it!

Lessons from Children

I learn a lot about trusting God with the outcome of specific circumstances in my life by watching the children around me. Ethan Hendon is the son of Cassandra, my niece, and her husband, Shawn. Born with a congenital defect called hypoplastic left heart syndrome, Ethan has an underdeveloped left side of his heart. His heart has only two chambers, not four. Though physically he is struggling, spiritually and mentally the little guy is thriving and making a tremendous difference in the lives of others.

Recently I found out that Ethan's school raised nearly $4,000 in his name for the American Heart Association. Not only will these funds help other children who are struggling with cardiovascular disease, but his indomitable optimism and faith-filled perspective have given other parents temporal and eternal hope. Ethan has been teaching me as well — and I believe his story will help you too. From the extraordinary life of six-year-old Ethan, every person can learn at least these five things about trusting God and turning our worries over to Him:

1. **Play the hand you're dealt.** Having been born with this condition, Ethan doesn't waste time complaining about what could be. Instead, he accepts his lot and trusts that his life is in the Lord's hands.

2. **You don't need music to dance.** Our energy may be

waning, but all we need is passion in our heart and mind in order to play and feel God's pleasure.

3. **Sometimes it's the interruption on our way to the main thing that is really the main thing.** After fifteen surgeries, Ethan has learned that schedules and plans are man's doing—not the Lord's.

4. **Life isn't easy, but God is always good.** We don't always have to understand what God is up to, but we do need to remember that He's always up to something good for those who love Him.

5. **Every day is a gift.** Are we going to treasure today and spend it well? Or will we fritter away our precious time in front of the television or the computer screen? Don't wait. Live the life God gave you—today!

Possibly the Best-Ever Use of a Tattoo

One of my colleagues recently found himself inside a greasy spoon burger joint one late-winter afternoon. His waitress, Debbie, was efficient and friendly. They struck up an easy conversation. As she placed a plate on the table, he noticed a distinctive-looking tattoo on her forearm. He couldn't see the whole design but saw the words "let God" just below the cuff of her long-sleeved T-shirt. He was intrigued.

"Is there a story behind your tattoo?" he asked.

A pool of tears suddenly appeared in Debbie's eyes. Yes, indeed there was a story behind it—and a dramatic one at that. She had been a drug addict hooked for years on a variety of illegal narcotics. At her lowest point, she had been introduced by a friend to Jesus Christ, and she had gone through an intensive faith-based rehabilitation program.

"My counselor urged me throughout the process," she shared, "to *let go and let God.*" After completing the program, Debbie found herself repeating that phrase over and over again. "Let go and let God" became the new theme of her once broken and now restored life.

"So I went out and got this tattoo," she said. "I had them place it on the exact spot where I used to inject myself with those wicked needles. Now if I ever get the urge to relapse, which has happened, I look down at my arm, and seeing that tattoo reminds me that God has changed my life and has rescued me from my addiction. Just looking at those words keeps me from spiraling down again."

I'm not suggesting we all run out and get a tattoo to help us remember that God is in charge of the world, but it is remarkable that this assurance can keep a former addict clean. The late American novelist Jack London reportedly said, "Show me a man with a tattoo and I'll show you a man with an interesting past." This would be true in Debbie's case, but because she found Jesus Christ, it's her present and future, not her past, that I find far more interesting, exciting, and redeeming.

This same assurance of a wonderful and exciting life can be yours — but only if you let go of your desire to control life and let God take you where He wants you to be.

Rest *in the Peace of God*

Surely the righteous will never be shaken;
    they will be remembered forever.
They will have no fear of bad news;
    their hearts are steadfast, trusting in the LORD.
Their hearts are secure, they will have no fear;
    in the end they will look in triumph on their foes.

PSALM 112:6–8

CAN YOU REMEMBER ANY INSTANCES IN WHICH YOU'VE SEEN the fear of a believer keeping them from being effective or from reflecting God's heart?

Many years ago I worked with Campus Crusade. On a quiet morning, our small department was meeting in a public area to study the Bible together. Suddenly a man stumbled (quite literally) through the door. He was obviously drunk, and the smell of his disheveled clothes gave evidence that he was most likely homeless. The group was stunned and a bit unsure of what to do. One of the women at the table, Margaret, became very scared. She may have been thinking that her life was in jeopardy. She began running around like a mouse was in the room. In this chaotic scene, she began to yell. "Get him out of here! Get him out of here!"

My colleague, John, was remarkably composed. He slowly stood up and approached the unannounced visitor. I'll never forget what he did. I was just twenty-two and eager to learn how to handle this type of situation. John gently reached out to the man and put his arm around him. "Let's go get you cleaned up," he suggested. "I know a place where you can get some sleep and they'll feed you a hot breakfast and provide a shower for you." And with that they were off.

That incident has never left me, and it serves as a metaphor for my understanding of how we are to minister to others and reflect the heart of Jesus.

If we want to be more like Jesus, we need to start acting more like Jesus. It's that simple — and that difficult. I encourage every Christian to tuck a copy of the Beatitudes in their pocket each morning before leaving the house. Better yet, memorize them. Internalize them. Meditate on them. Begin to see your place in the world through the lens of Jesus' own words:

> Blessed are the poor in spirit,
> for theirs is the kingdom of heaven.
> Blessed are those who mourn,
> for they will be comforted.
> Blessed are the meek,
> for they will inherit the earth.
> Blessed are those who hunger and thirst for
> righteousness,
> for they will be filled.
> Blessed are the merciful,
> for they will be shown mercy.
> Blessed are the pure in heart,
> for they will see God.
> Blessed are the peacemakers,
> for they will be called children of God.

Blessed are those who are persecuted because
of righteousness,
for theirs is the kingdom of heaven.

MATTHEW 5:3 – 10

The Lord always gives a choice. Jesus stands at the door and knocks. He doesn't force Himself on us. We don't *have* to open the door. We can choose to open or to ignore. That's our privilege as created beings. But if we answer, engage, and accept His invitation, we will rest in the peace of God.

Writing to his son Christopher, J.R.R. Tolkien offered the following chilling, though transparent, observation:

> We all long for [Eden], and we are constantly glimpsing it:
> *our whole nature* at its best and least corrupted, its gentlest
> and most humane, *is still soaked with the sense of "exile."*
> If you come to think of it, your (very just) horror at the
> stupid murder of the hawk, and your obstinate memory of
> this "home" of yours in an idyllic hour (when often there
> is an illusion of the stay of time and decay and a sense of
> gentle peace) ... are derived from Eden.[1]

At the risk of overstating the reality of our current cultural circumstances, I'm inclined to suggest that this creeping and haunting "sense of 'exile' " sits at the center of much of our misery and discontent, both individually and collectively. Since Adam and Eve's exile from the garden, life on earth has been an uphill grind. Things just don't seem to work out the way we think they should. Even for those who don't accept as true Jesus Christ's redemptive sacrifice on our behalf on the cross, there is a sense that something is terribly wrong with the world. In response to the unrelieved monotony of strain and struggle, we expend our energies on worldly and temporary endeavors. What we're really doing is trying to fill the "God-shaped vacuum" with everything from money to sex to alcohol to power and the accumulation of possessions. In the process, we often lie to ourselves. After all, motives are easily disguised. At times, even behavior carried out under the guise of ministry or general goodwill has as its motive the feeding and strok-ing of our flagging egos and fragile self-esteem. Consciously or subconsciously, we think one more thing will bring happi-ness. Uncomfortable with the lack of control over their lives, some may eagerly grab hold of a powerful or influential posi-tion, whether in politics, business, or even church. It feels good to be the boss — and it may even seem noble. But if we do this because we think the move will make us happy and satisfy our appetite to be somebody and gain a reputation for doing some great thing, we will inevitably be disappointed.

This quest to fill the aching void and nurse the sickness created by original sin is not limited to professional or even social circles. In fact, it almost always first manifests itself at home and in the family. We may become dissatisfied with our spouse, thinking he or she just isn't doing it for us anymore, but someone else surely will. Or perhaps we find ourselves turn-ing into a tyrant with our own children, or ignoring them all together. Either way, a sense of selfishness grabs hold of us. In the quest to rescue ourselves from exile, we begin to think and act as though everything revolves around us. We bury ourselves in work or fill our calendars with a host of obligations. These endeavors make us feel needed and important. Busyness acts like a balm on a burn — but the cooling and calming sensation only lasts so long. Any relief from the "exile" is temporary, and we soon find ourselves adrift and discontented. We want more. That which promised to deliver didn't — and may have left us more jaded in the long term. The vicious cycle begins anew.

In a recent article in *The New York Times*, Bethany Patchin, a thirty-two-year-old divorced mother of four from Nashville, Tennessee, shared with readers her theological confusion. When Ms. Patchin was eighteen years of age, she wrote an essay for *Boundless*, Focus on the Family's web-based magazine for twentysomethings, in which she supported the idea of courtship and a commitment not to kiss before marriage. She expressed love and devotion for Jesus. She would later coauthor a book with her then-husband Sam Torode, advocating natural family planning and voicing strong opposition to contraception, citing the authority of Scripture. Now years later, she isn't so sure, not only about contraception, but about the biggest issues in life. The blows of life have taken their toll on her. "Where I'm at now, it's confusing," Ms. Patchin reflected. "One day I am like, 'Sure, God exists and loves all of us,' and the next day I am like, 'No, I don't think so.' I think that's healthy. Agnosticism is a healthy part of any good faith."[2]

What happened? I've never met Bethany Patchin, but the progression of her journey is not unfamiliar based on the people I talk with and the letters we receive at Focus. She is reeling and struggling to find her moral center. She is expressing an honest heart — and God wants us to have honest hearts. There is nothing wrong with asking questions. But in her time of searching, she is allowing the world's values to shape and influence her values, a habit warned against by the apostle Paul in his letter to the first-century church at Corinth, which had been experiencing division among its members. In the angst he observed in their letters to him, Paul recognized the cause: believers were bringing the spirit of the city of Corinth into the church instead of bringing the spirit of the church into the city.

The Bottom Line of Bottom Lines

To a significant degree, this habit that plays out day after day in our society compelled me to write this book. Our problems are rooted in Adam and Eve's expulsion from the garden, of course, but they're being exacerbated by people who should know better. Christians who fail to reflect God's heart often do so because they've chosen to believe the world's great lies. I share this not with a haughty spirit but a contrite one. I also fail at doing the right thing — all too often, in fact. I am mindful of it and want to do better each time I fail.

But many of us seem convinced that the things of this world can fill the void that only Christ Himself is capable of adequately satisfying. Instead of bringing the spirit of Christ's church into the world, we're bringing the world and all its problems into the church. How else can we explain such disturbing trends as the high rate of divorce among Christians or the increasing number of out-of-wedlock births or the use of pornography, among even clergy? And what of those who claim to be followers of Jesus yet trample others in their pursuit of power, position, and prestige?

I am left to believe one sad and troubling thing: many of us aren't really sure that Jesus meant what He said when He said what He meant — that He is "the way and the truth and the life" (John 14:6). Many of us are not embracing Paul's assurances that "the foolishness of God is wiser than human wisdom, and the weakness of God is stronger than human strength" (1 Corinthians 1:25) and that "God chose the foolish things of the world to shame the wise; God chose the weak things of the world to shame the strong. God chose the lowly things of this world and the despised things — and the things that are not — to nullify the things that are, so that no one may boast before him" (1:27 – 29).

We are continually auditioning for a role that Christ has already won for us, and exhausting ourselves and others in the process. We are desperate in our effort to rescue ourselves from this exile that Tolkien referred to, subconsciously believing that all will be well just as soon as we do well on our own behalf — whether in words or deeds.

Getting to the Heart of Human Desire

In chapter 6, I pointed to some signs of pride and arrogance. In revisiting those comments, I'm reminded of Tim Keller's powerful chapter, "The Seduction of Success," in his book *Counterfeit Gods*. Keller reflects on the rising culture of competition, as well as on our chronic and seemingly insatiable appetite for approval and applause:

> The human heart's desire for a particular valuable object (human affirmation) may be conquered, but its need to have some such object is unconquerable. How can we break our heart's fixation on doing "some great thing" in order to heal ourselves of our sense of inadequacy, in order to give our lives meaning? Only when we see what

Jesus, our great Suffering Servant, has done for us will we finally understand why God's salvation does not require us to do "some great thing." We don't have to do it, because Jesus has.[3]

Since the fall of Adam and Eve, the human heart has always sought approval in the wrong people, places, and things. In fact, many of us will do almost anything for it — whether lying, cheating, gossiping, manipulating, stealing, or even murdering.

The bottom line is this: It is only Christ who can tame and rein in this runaway spirit of worldly desire. It is only in and through Him that we can truly find satisfaction and healing for our broken hearts.

The Great Eucatastrophe

In 1939, J.R.R. Tolkien prepared an essay to be delivered as a lecture at the University of St Andrews in Scotland. It was titled "On Fairy-Stories," and in the piece he explained and defended the use of fantasy as a literary form.[4] The entire work is worth reading, but one part in particular speaks to our current state of affairs — and in a most hopeful way. According to Tolkien, we're naturally drawn to stories, of course, but we're especially drawn to drama and tales with a sudden, happy ending. In the reflection, though, Tolkien coined an interesting term: *eucatastrophe* — the joyful (*eu*) catastrophe. I find his insights fascinating and share in his own words the deeply theological motivation behind *eucatastrophe*:

> I coined the word "*eucatastrophe*": the sudden happy turn in a story which pierces you with a joy that brings tears

(which I argued it is the highest function of fairy-stories to produce). And I was there led to the view that it produces its peculiar effect because it is a sudden glimpse of Truth, your whole nature chained in material cause and effect, the chain of death, feels a sudden relief as if a major limb out of joint had suddenly snapped back. It perceives — if the story has literary "truth" on the second plane (for which see the essay) — that this is indeed how things really do work in the Great World for which our nature is made. And I concluded by saying that the Resurrection was the greatest "*eucatastrophe*" possible in the greatest Fairy Story — and produces that essential emotion: Christian joy which produces tears because it is qualitatively so like sorrow, because it comes from those places where Joy and Sorrow are at one, reconciled, as selfishness and altruism are lost in Love.[5]

In his inimitable way, Tolkien assures us that in the end, despite every appearance to the contrary, all is well. Why else would we call even the worst day in all of time and space, the day Jesus of Nazareth died, "Good Friday"? Because in the end, the God of the universe has promised to make all things new. "Write this down," John wrote in Revelation, "for these words are trustworthy and true" (Revelation 21:5).

Do you find this as reassuring as I do? In a generation in which hype has become habit and there is no shortage of bad news, the message of the gospel is "good news" indeed. For those who believe and place their trust in the Lord, they need not grow anxious or cower in fear about this coming age. Yes, we must prepare and brace ourselves for any host of troubles that infiltrate a broken world — but preparation is not the same thing as worry. Dr. D. Martyn-Lloyd Jones, a former physician familiar with the ways in which anxiety can ravage a person's health, offered a practical fix for this bad habit:

> Why do you allow yourself to be worried thus about the future?... Worry about the future is so utterly futile and useless; it achieves nothing at all. We are very slow to see that; yet how true it is. Indeed we can go further and say that worry is never of any value at all. This is seen with particular clarity as you come to face the future. Apart from anything else, it is a pure waste of energy because however much you worry you cannot do anything about it. In any case its threatened catastrophes are imaginary; they are not certain, they may never happen at all ...
>
> We must not go forward and tack tomorrow's quota on to today's, otherwise it may be too much for us. We have to take it day by day ...
>
> If you want to go through life without crippling yourself and burdening yourself and perhaps losing your health and the control of your nerves, these are the cardinal rules. Do not carry yesterday or tomorrow with you; live for today and for the twelve hours you are in.[6]

Working toward Shalom or the Flourishing of the Culture

I admire the discipline, wisdom, and insight of Tim Keller, whose influential teachings are reflected within these pages. I lean on his perspective one last time for the simple reason that he has a measured and practical sense on where many Christians are in their pursuit of living lives that reflect God's heart.

The relationship of Christians to culture is the singular current crisis point for the church. Evangelicals are deeply divided over how to interact with a social order that is growing increasingly post-Christian. Some advise a reemphasis on tradition and on "letting the church be the church," rejecting any direct attempt to influence society as a whole. Others are hostile to culture, but hopeful that they can change it through aggressive action, often of a political sort. Still others believe that "you change culture one heart at a time." Finally, many are attracted to the new culture and want to reengineer the church to modify its adversarial relationship with culture. Many in the "one heart at a time" party play down doctrine and stress experience, while some in the reengineering group are changing distinctives of evangelical doctrine in the name of cultural engagement. That is fueling much theological controversy, but even people who agree on the need for change disagree over what to *do* to our doctrine to reach the culture.

None of the strategies listed above should be abandoned. We need Christian tradition, Christians in politics, and effective evangelism. And the church has always contextualized itself into its surrounding culture. There are harmful excesses in every approach, however. I think that is because many have turned their specialty into a single magic bullet that will solve the whole problem. I doubt such a magic bullet exists, but just bundling them all together is not sufficient either.[7]

I agree with Tim that the secret is found not in strategy but in attitude. We are called to demonstrate the love of Christ to the world. That's the important thing. It's not a means to an end, but it has to be the reason. Our duty as Christians is never to abandon what is right. Even though the environment may be very much against us, we can't think of our mission as a lost cause. We should never give up articulating the truths of Scripture, even if the culture doesn't agree. We have to continue to stand for what we believe, no matter what happens.

Although recent votes on the issue of same-sex marriage have been overwhelmingly supportive of traditional marriage (thirty-two out of thirty-two states have voted to protect marriage), shifts have occurred in some places. Same-sex marriage is now legal in a handful of states because judges or legislators have decreed it. From a Christian perspective, it is important to understand that there is a clear biblical definition of marriage: a union between one man and one woman. Jesus Himself mentions it as He cites the Genesis definition: "A man will leave his father and mother and be united to his wife, and the two will become one flesh" (Matthew 19:5, citing Genesis 2:24). It's clear.

Even where there hasn't been spiritual illumination, it seems that every culture gets this. They get married, in some form or fashion. Marriage serves a benefit to the culture. It is utilitarian at the very least that women and men procreate and make the next generation of children. Marriage has played a role in every civilization. Then Jesus comes on the scene and reinforces from a Judeo-Christian standpoint that this is an institution created by God.

Many supporters of same-sex marriage object to the fact that most of us in the Christian community support traditional marriage. We're just trying to live out the tenets of our faith.

We see it clearly stated in the Bible that marriage is between one man and one woman. So people who have an issue with that have, in reality, an issue with the Scriptures. I understand that cultural mores can change, but we're still going to speak truth from our perspective regarding the biblical model of marriage. At the same time, I am hopeful that those who oppose traditional marriage will come to understand the wisdom and design God intended. Ultimately, the goal is that everyone will know Jesus Christ and embrace His teaching. We must be careful not to create a "super sin" out of homosexuality. It is one expression of a person's brokenness before God along with many others that affect even larger segments of our society. No matter what form of self-centeredness grips us — adultery, homosexuality, lying, cheating, gossiping, pride (and the list goes on) — we all need God's redemption through Jesus Christ.

Father, into Your Hands I Commit My Spirit

I recently learned that at the time of Jesus' crucifixion, Jewish parents would typically teach and recite with their child a single prayer at bedtime — Psalm 31:5: "Into your hands I commit my spirit; redeem me, O Lord, the God of truth" (NIV, 1984 edition). I found it interesting that Jesus' final statement on the cross was this very same prayer parents were saying with their children — with only the word "Father" added to it. This fact prompted the theologian William Barclay to observe that "Jesus died with a prayer on his lips."[8]

We know from Scripture that at the moment of Jesus' death, many supernatural things occurred: the curtain in the temple was torn in two (Luke 23:45); the earth shook; rocks shattered and split; many "holy people" even rose from the dead and appeared to many people in the city of Jerusalem (Matthew 27:51–53).

Amazing! What a moment! It sounds like an implausible scene from a high-budget Hollywood production. But unlike fabricated and fictional events projected in a movie theater, these events actually happened as recorded. From that supernatural moment we can learn much from this final statement of Jesus from the cross.

Bible scholars tell us these final words were uttered as a ram's horn, a shofar, was being blown to signal the beginning of Passover and also to mark the time to begin slaughtering lambs for the festival. It also fulfilled the Scriptures, reflecting the very moment that John the Baptist had prophesied when he referred to Jesus as the Lamb being led to slaughter: "Look, the Lamb of God, who takes away the sin of the world!" (John 1:29).

Although Jesus' words are directed to His Father, the public and loud nature of the communication tells us they are meant for those witnessing the event — and for you and me as well. In fact, Jesus doesn't need to speak audibly in order to be heard by His Father. But He is clearly sending a message to those within earshot. Here is Jesus, hanging on the cross in front of His executioners. And in the final act of His life, He is telling the power brokers that despite their best efforts, He has won the final victory. They haven't defeated Him. They are succeeding in killing His body, but not His soul. His relationship with His Father is now restored after the unspeakable agony of abandonment by the Father (Matthew 27:46) as Jesus bore the sin of the world.

The boldness of Jesus' final act should embolden us. Are we willing to speak openly about our faith? Are we willing to lean on the promise and power of the Scriptures and live boldly for Jesus? In whom do we find our rest? In whom do we place our trust? As we see Jesus hanging on the cross, we are reminded that His sacrifice was personal and painful — and He offered Himself willingly for you and for me.

This is the end of the greatest story ever told — the story of the greatest man who ever lived. Or is it the end? Of course not! What happened on Good Friday was a tragedy, to be sure, but a tragedy with a twist and certainly not the end of the story. It was, in fact, a joyful catastrophe. It is this reality that shines the light of ultimate perspective on our work in the world.

We Are All in the Boat Together

As this chapter and book draw to a close, I am reminded of Rembrandt's famous painting, *The Storm on the Sea of Galilee.** It was the legendary painter's only seascape, and it dramatically captures the moment right before Jesus calms the turbulent waters (Mark 4:35 – 40). It's an exquisite piece of art for several reasons, and an appropriate one to point to at this time in our history.

If you were to examine the painting, you would notice there are fourteen people in the boat. This is a curious thing, especially since Mark's account reveals that Jesus and the twelve disciples are in the vessel. Who is the fourteenth person? Rembrandt painted himself in the boat — intended, I believe, to emphasize that we're all in the boat together. We're all being

---

* Note: This famous painting was stolen in 1990 from the Isabella Stewart Gardner Museum in Boston, Massachusetts, and has never been found.

tossed about by the waves, constantly confronting the danger-
ous tide of the world's sins and imperfections. Yet, because
Jesus is in the boat with us, we have nothing to fear, as long as
we put our faith in Him.

Let All Things Seen and Unseen— Their Notes in Gladness Blend

Until a stroke rendered her unable to speak, Holocaust survivor
Corrie ten Boom traveled the country to share the remarkable
and heart-wrenching story of her experience in Nazi-controlled
Holland during World War II, which included time in a con-
centration camp. Prior to their capture, Corrie's father secretly
hid Jewish refugees in their home. His explanation for why
he was willing to risk his life for others serves as a metaphor
for Christian life today. "In this household," Casper ten Boom
declared, "God's people are always welcome."[9] Corrie was the
family's sole survivor, and her testimony moved and inspired
thousands of people. When she spoke, she hung a rather unat-
tractive tapestry next to the podium and offered no explanation
until the conclusion of her message. At that point she turned
the fabric around, revealing a magnificent work of art. She concluded by reading the poem titled "The Weaver," which serves
as the ideal benediction for this book. As Corrie ten Boom
would remind us, truly there is more to life than meets the eye.

The Weaver

My life is but a weaving
Between my Lord and me,
I cannot choose the colors
He worketh steadily.
Oft times He weaveth sorrow
And I, in foolish pride
Forget He sees the upper
And I, the under side.
Not til the loom is silent
And the shuttles cease to fly
Shall God unroll the canvas
And explain the reason why.
The dark threads are as needful
In the Weaver's skillful hand
As the threads of gold and silver
In the pattern He has planned.
He knows, He loves, He cares,
Nothing this truth can dim.
He gives His very best to those
Who chose to walk with Him.[10]

Acknowledgments

ALL BOOKS ARE THE PRODUCT OF THE LIVES THAT TOUCH the writer, and *ReFocus* is certainly no different. Over the years, this message has taken hold of me, and I appreciate the many people who helped pull these thoughts from my heart and mind and transfer them to the printed page. My dearest confidante of all, my wife, Jean, is my sounding board and filter. She is most deserving of all. Without her wisdom and feedback, the work would be incomplete. My colleague, friend, and collaborator, Paul Batura, is blessed with a knack for helping me say things just so and for pulling together volumes of research into digestible and practical doses. The talented and visionary team at Zondervan, led by Cindy Lambert, Dirk Buursma, and Amanda Sorenson, helped refine and sharpen themes. I am grateful for the collective and individual wisdom of the members of Focus on the Family's board of directors. Over the years they have counseled and encouraged me and provided invaluable mentoring. Other individuals who have contributed in various ways include colleagues Joel Vaughan, Patty Watkins, Sue McFadden, Tim Goeglein, Gary Schneeberger, and my friend and agent, Wes Yoder.

Finally, I am deeply indebted to the countless people whose words, works, and godly examples have served to model the essence of what I have attempted to convey throughout the pages of this book — that the Lord wants us to draw nearer to Him and to live lives that reflect His heart, not the ways of the world.

Notes

CHAPTER 1: Time for a Change

1. "Man in the Mirror," lyrics by Siedah Garrett and Glen Ballard; recorded by Michael Jackson (Epic Records, 1988).

CHAPTER 2: The Clash of Two Worlds

1. See "The Edict of Milan: Constantine Augustus and Licinius Augustus," http://gbgm-umc.org/umw/bible/milan.stm (accessed May 21, 2012).

2. Marcus Dods, ed., *The Works of Aurelius Augustine* (Edinburgh: T&T Clark, 1871), 47.

3. Quoted in A. D. Cousins and Damien Grace, eds., *A Companion to Thomas More* (Madison, N.J.: Fairleigh Dickinson University Press, 2009), 31.

4. Cited in Billy Graham, *Just as I Am: The Autobiography of Billy Graham* (New York: HarperCollins, 1997), 529.

5. Ibid.

6. Ibid., 530.

7. Ibid., 191.

8. Timothy Keller, foreword to Michael Gerson and Peter Wehner, *City of Man: Religion and Politics in a New Era* (Chicago: Moody, 2010), 11.

9. See David VanDrunen, *Living in God's Two Kingdoms: A Biblical Vision for Christianity and Culture* (Wheaton, Ill.: Crossway, 2010), 14.

10. See William J. Wright, *Martin Luther's Understanding of God's Two Kingdoms: A Response to the Challenge of Skepticism* (Grand Rapids: Baker, 2010), 33.

11. Personal correspondence, 2011.

12. Personal correspondence, 2011.

CHAPTER 3: **Don't Panic**

1. Henry Wadsworth Longfellow, "The Theologian's Tale; The Legend Beautiful," www.hwlongfellow.org/poems_poem.php?pid=2064 (accessed May 22, 2012).

2. Naphtali Lewis, *Life in Egypt under Roman Rule* (Oxford: Oxford University Press, 1985), 54.

3. Aaron Milavec, *The Didache: Text, Translation, Analysis, and Commentary* (Collegeville, Minn.: Liturgical Press, 2003), 5.

4. Ezra Pound, *Make it New: Essays* (New Haven, Conn.: Yale University Press, 1935).

5. Mark Noll, *America's God: From Jonathan Edwards to Abraham Lincoln* (New York: Oxford University Press, 2002), 437.

CHAPTER 4: **Fan or Follower?**

1. Quoted in Josephine Vivaldo, "Are You a Follower or Fan of Jesus?" *Christian Post* (May 17, 2011), www.christianpost.com/news/are-you-a-fan-or-follower-of-jesus-50267/ (accessed May 23, 2012).

2. William Byron Forbush, ed., *Fox's Book of Martyrs: A History of the Lives, Sufferings, and Deaths of the Early Christian and Protestant Martyrs* (Grand Rapids: Zondervan, 2009), 36–37.

3. Ibid., 37.

4. Charles Spurgeon, *Evening by Evening: The Devotions of Charles Spurgeon* (Wheaton, Ill.: Crossway, 2007), 169.

CHAPTER 5: Taking the Long View of Life

1. Cited in Rowland Croucher, "Malcolm Muggeridge on Mother Teresa," http://jmm.aaa.net.au/articles/4746.htm (accessed May 24, 2012).

2. Malcolm Muggeridge, *Something Beautiful for God: The Classic Account of Mother Teresa's Journey into Compassion* (New York: Harper, 1971), 31.

3. Cited in William J. Bausch, *A World of Stories for Preachers and Teachers* (Mystic, Conn.: Twenty-Third Publications, 1998), 362.

4. Quoted in Peter Kreeft, *Christianity for Modern Pagans: Pascal's Pensées* (San Francisco: Ignatius, 1993), 158.

5. C. S. Lewis, *Mere Christianity* (1943; repr., New York: Macmillan, 1981), 79.

6. A. W. Tozer, *The Pursuit of God* (Harrisburg, Pa.: Christian Publications, 1948), 73.

7. Ray Vander Laan, "Zealots – People of the Palm Branch," http://www.followtherabbi.com/thepeopleofthepalmbranch/http://followtherabbi.com/guide/detail/zealots-people-of-the-palm-branch (accessed May 22, 2012).

8. See Ray Vander Laan, *Echoes of His Presence* (Grand Rapids: Zondervan, 1998), 147–48.

9. Quoted in Walter Hooper, ed., *The Collected Letters of C. S. Lewis: Narnia, Cambridge, and Joy 1950–1963* (San Francisco: HarperSanFrancisco, 2007), 3:147.

CHAPTER 6: **Always Be Ready!**

1. Timothy J. Keller, "The Advent of Humility," *Christianity Today* 52 (December 2008): 50 – 53, www.christianitytoday.com/ct/2008/december/20.51.html (accessed May 24, 2012).

2. Quoted in Berta Delgado, "Pastor Known to Millions through His Books," *Dallas Morning News* (January 2, 2001).

3. Ibid.

4. William Jenkyn and James Sherman, *An Exposition Upon the Epistle of Jude Delivered in Christ-Church, London* (Edinburgh: Nichol, 1865), 137.

5. Francis A. Schaeffer, *A Christian Manifesto* (Wheaton, Ill.: Crossway, 1981).

6. Francis A. Schaeffer, *Death in the City* (Downers Grove, Ill.: InterVarsity, 1969).

7. Andy Stanley, "The Separation of Church and Hate" (July 3, 2011), www.northpoint.org/messages/the-separation-of-church-and-hate (accessed May 24, 2012).

8. C. S. Lewis, *Mere Christianity* (1943; repr., New York: Macmillan, 1981), 104.

CHAPTER 7: **No One Is Beyond the Reach of God**

1. Richard J. Mouw, *Uncommon Decency: Christian Civility in an Uncivil World* (Downers Grove, Ill.: InterVarsity, 1992), 55.

2. "Douglas Bruce Kicks Photographer during Swearing-In Ceremony," www.thedenverchannel.com/news/15042134/detail.html (accessed May 22, 2012).

3. "Focus on the Family – CS *Indy* Partner to Support Foster Families," *KKTV* (May 9, 2011), www.kktv.com/home/headlines/Focus_on_the_Family_-_CS_Indy_Partner_to_Support_Foster_Families_121547674.html (accessed May 25, 2012).

4. J. Adrian Stanley, "Long Story Short," Colorado Springs *Independent* (June 9, 2011), www.csindy.com/colorado/long-story-short/Content?oid=2244142 (accessed May 22, 2012).

5. Bob Kellogg, "Focus: 'We need to band together,'" July 4, 2012, www.onenewsnow.com/Culture/Default.aspx?id=1625610 (accessed August 20, 2012).

CHAPTER 8: **Don't Be a Miserable Christian**

1. Brennan Manning, *The Ragamuffin Gospel* (Sisters, Ore.: Multnomah, 2000), 88.

2. William Wordsworth, *The Poetical Works of William Wordsworth* (Oxford: Clarendon, 1940), 275.

3. D. Martyn Lloyd-Jones, *Studies in the Sermon on the Mount* (Grand Rapids: Eerdmans, 1976), 2:256.

4. Thomas Fuller, *The Wisdom of Our Fathers: Selections from the Writings of Thomas Fuller* (London: Religious Tract Society, 1865), 298.

5. Quoted in Dan Wooding, "The Jesus People Revolution," *Assist Ministries* (January 5, 2012), www.assistnews.net/Stories/2012/s12010031.htm (accessed May 25, 2012).

6. Nora Holm, *The Runner's Bible* (New York: Houghton Mifflin, 1913), 33.

CHAPTER 9: **Scripture as the Rock**

1. Quoted in William J. Stern, "How Dagger John Saved New York's Irish," *City Journal* (Spring 1997), www.city-journal.org/html/7_2_a2.html (accessed May 25, 2012).

2. Ibid.

3. Ibid.

4. Ibid.

5. "Four Spiritual Laws," www.campuscrusade.com/fourlawseng.htm (accessed May 25, 2012).

6. Peggy Noonan, "We Need a Ronald Reagan," *Wall Street Journal* (July 9, 2011), http://online.wsj.com/article/SB10001424052702303 365804576432282516405752.html (accessed May 25, 2012).

7. Cited in *The Parliamentary History of England from the Earliest Period to the Year 1803* (London: Hansard, 1817), 278.

8. Marshall McLuhan, *Understanding Media: The Extensions of Man* (New York: McGraw-Hill, 1964), 7.

9. Alice Fryling, *The Art of Spiritual Listening: Responding to God's Voice Amid the Noise of Life* (Colorado Springs: WaterBrook, 2009), 7.

10. Thom S. Rainer and Jess W. Rainer, *The Millennials: Connecting to America's Largest Generation* (Nashville: Broadman and Holman, 2011).

CHAPTER 10: **The Kindness of God Leads to Repentance**

1. Flannery O'Connor, *A Good Man Is Hard to Find* (New Brunswick, N.J.: Rutgers University Press, 1993).

CHAPTER 11: **We're Not Entitled to Run the World**

1. Ernst Falzeder and Eva Brabant, eds., *The Correspondence of Sigmund Freud and Sándor Ferenczi: Volume 2: 1914–1919* (Cambridge, Mass.: Harvard University Press, 1996), 729; see Judith Shulevitz, "Bring Back the Sabbath," *New York Times* magazine (March 2, 2003), www.nytimes.com/2003/03/02/ magazine/bring-back-the-sabbath.html?pagewanted=all&src=pm (accessed May 29, 2012).

2. Quoted in Erin Roach, "'Adrianisms' Captures Notable Sayings of Adrian Rogers," *Baptist Press* (July 6, 2006), www.bpnews.net/ bpnews.asp?ID=23591 (accessed May 29, 2012).

CHAPTER 12: **Rest in the Peace of God**

1. Quoted in Humphrey Carpenter, ed., *The Letters of J.R.R. Tolkien* (New York: Houghton Mifflin, 1981), 125, www.e-reading.org .ua/bookreader.php/139008/The_Letters_of_J.R.R.Tolkien.pdf (accessed May 30, 2012).

2. Quoted in Mark Oppenheimer, "An Evolving View of Natural Family Planning," *New York Times* (July 8, 2011), www.nytimes .com/2011/07/09/us/09beliefs.html (accessed May 29, 2012).

3. Timothy Keller, *Counterfeit Gods: The Empty Promises of Money, Sex, and Power, and the Only Hope that Matters* (New York: Dutton, 2000), 93.

4. J.R.R. Tolkien, *Tree and Leaf* (New York: HarperCollins, 2001).

5. Quoted in Carpenter, ed., *Letters of J.R.R. Tolkien*, 115–16, www.e-reading.org.ua/bookreader.php/139008/The_Letters_ of_J.R.R.Tolkien.pdf (accessed May 30, 2012).

6. D. Martyn Lloyd-Jones, *Studies in the Sermon on the Mount* (Grand Rapids: Eerdmans, 1971), 2:416–18.

7. Timothy J. Keller, "A New Kind of Urban Christian: As the City Goes, So Goes the Culture," *Christianity Today* 50 (May 1, 2006): 33–36.

8. William Barclay, *We Have Seen the Lord!: The Passion and Resurrection of Jesus Christ* (Louisville, Ky.: Westminster John Knox, 1998), 106.

9. Corrie ten Boom, *The Hiding Place*, 35th anniv. ed. (1971; repr., Grand Rapids: Baker, 2006), 94.

10. The poem "The Weaver" is attributed to Grand Colfax Tullar, composer of many popular hymns and hymnals, www.boltonct history.org/granttullar.html (accessed May 22, 2012).

About Jim Daly

Jim Daly is president and CEO of Focus on the Family and host of its National Radio Hall of Fame–honored daily broadcast, heard by more than 2.9 million listeners a week on more than one thousand radio stations across the United States.

Daly's personal journey from orphan to head of an international Christian organization dedicated to helping families thrive is a powerful story. Abandoned by his alcoholic father at age five, Daly lost his mother to cancer four years later—a wound deepened when his grieving stepfather emptied the family home and took off with almost everything while Daly, the youngest of five children, and his siblings were at their mother's funeral.

After being in foster care, Daly became a Christian in high school and found meaning, purpose, and a sense of belonging.

Daly assumed the presidency of Focus on the Family in 2005. He began his career at Focus in 1989 as an assistant to the president. In 2004, he was appointed chief operating officer, the role he held until he was handpicked by founder Dr. James Dobson to be the ministry's president.

Daly has received the 2008 World Children's Center Humanitarian Award, the 2009 Children's Hunger Fund Children's Champion Award, and the 2010 HomeWord Family Ministry Award. He is a regular panelist for *The Washington Post/Newsweek* blog "On Faith," and his own blog, "Finding Home," appears daily on the Focus on the Family online community (www.focusonlinecommunities.com/blogs/Finding_Home).

Daly is the author of three books: *ReFocus*, *Stronger*, and *Finding Home*. He and his wife, Jean, have two children and live in Colorado Springs.

About Paul Batura

Paul J. Batura is a senior writer to the president of Focus on the Family and the author of several biographies, including *Good Day! The Paul Harvey Story*. He and his wife, Julie, live in Colorado Springs with their three young sons, Riley Hamilton, Will Connolly, and Alexander James.

From the Publisher

GREAT BOOKS

ARE EVEN BETTER WHEN THEY'RE SHARED!

Help other readers find this one:

- Post a review at your favorite online bookseller

- Post a picture on a social media account and share why you enjoyed it

- Send a note to a friend who would also love it—or better yet, give them a copy

Thanks for reading!

Printed in the USA
CPSIA information can be obtained
at www.ICGtesting.com
JSHW031134070823
46073JS00013B/526